What Was Taken

an untold story

Carol Haack

(The young girl who survived to write this account)

Copyright © 2018 Carol Haack
Honoring Girls Press LLC

All rights reserved. No part of this book may be reproduced or stored or transmitted by any means, including photocopying, without the written permission of the copyright holder. Translation in any language is prohibited without the permission of the copyright holder.

Publisher's Cataloging-in-Publication data
Haack, Carol.
What was Taken : an untold story / Carol Haack.
281 pg., 23 cm.
ISBN 978-0-6920918-2-1
1. Serial murderers—Minnesota—Minneapolis—Fiction.
2. Serial murderers—Minnesota—Austin—Fiction.
3. Serial murderers—Minnesota—Rochester—Fiction.
4. Serial murderers—Michigan—Grand Rapids—Fiction.
5. Crime in literature. I. Haack, Carol.

PS3606.A727 W438 2018

ISBN 978-0-692-09182-1
Honoring Girls Press LLC

Book Design by Jim Bisakowski, http://bookdesign.ca

Printed in USA

For my fourth grade teacher,
Edith Morey (1925-2013)

Your inspiration lives on
in every life you touched.

Author's Note

What Was Taken is a fictionalized account of my real life story of abduction by serial killer David James Torgerson, whose path crossed mine when I was just ten years old.

Although based on true events, my personal experience and extensive research, the narrative's internal thoughts, dialogue, character motivations and intentions have been created from my imagination.

Each crime scene has been grounded by facts gathered from the following sources: Minneapolis police reports; Olmstead County Sheriff records; Grand Rapids, Michigan, police recordings; courthouse transcripts from Mower and Olmstead County Courts in Minnesota as well as personal interviews with sisters of each murdered girl.

Chronological List of Victims

- Unnamed Young girls (4)
- Carol Haack, age 10
- Female patient RSMS
- Female patient RSMS
- ABC worker
- Charlotte Jarrett, age 29
- Linda Wandrus, age 18
- Julie Mehrman, age 19
- Rebecca Hanson, age 19
- Anne Hogan, age 20,
- Lana Torgerson, age 23
- Rebecca Rathbun, age, 14
- Sylvia Torgerson, age 3
- John Torgerson, age 1
- Susan Scott, age 23

Part One

Words can make a deeper scar than silence can heal.
						~Unknown

Carol Haack July 12, 1959

> I stopped and picked up one of her white sandals. After stuffing it into my front jean pocket, I headed for home.

Like a cicada burrowing through dirt, up, up I climbed until my eyes opened to a world spinning out of control. "Momma, Momma, Momma I want to go home," I begged of the empty space. "Let go," I told myself. "Just another bad dream, fall back, sleep, sleep..."

In time, my eyes scrunched open again. My lips cracked like the hide of my mom's crocodile purse as I tugged them apart. When I poked the tip of my swollen tongue across them, they tasted metallic and salty. I was thirsty, oh so thirsty. According to our church, at ten years of age I had reached the age of reason but there was nothing reasonable about my predicament. Even though my family never prayed, I bargained: Lord have mercy. And then sorrow twisted me back into the darkness.

My hands floated up to my bloated face. Their motion roused me. Brittle blood caked my cheeks and chin. Lifting my head, I saw blood, the color and consistency of smashed blueberries, pooled on my exposed midriff. Gnats, chiggers, and relentless Minnesota mosquitoes flitted around me. I tried to swat them away but my hands were clumsy. A barbed wire fence, slung out over a ravine fifty feet above Turtle Creek, held me as if I were suspended in a lazy hammock. I rocked back and forth to soothe myself, pushing its barbs deeper into my skin. My thighs twitched.

I shook my head from side-to-side. Drawing a boxer's breath, I tilted my body sideways. Anchoring my left knee deep into the dirt, I reached up and grabbed a gnarled tree root just above my head. Using all of my strength, I pulled my body close to the rise. After forcing my right leg over the ledge, I tucked and rolled landing on my back. My eyes twitched and burned as I watched the day's amber heat circle into lavender. When the sun started to set, a chill crawled up my body.

"Stand up. You must stand up," I told myself. My pulse quickened, my temples pounded, and my feet wobbled. Surprise swallowed me whole when my head and chest flopped down past my waist like a limp Raggedy Ann doll. Sweat puddled around the waistband of my red shorts, my arms swayed, and my knuckles dangled across dew-soaked leaves on the forest floor. I dropped with the first step and then I crawled like a baby until my knees gave way. Still I moved forward, pulling my chest along with my forearms and shimmying my hips. Shivers stole up and down my spine even as beads of sweat formed on my brow and upper lip.

"Don't give up," I said to myself as I shoved forward. "You are almost out of the woods." Finally, I saw it: glints of caramel, the yellow road leading home. But a deep ditch separated me from it. I was worn out, down for the count. Suddenly my mother's voice hammered in my head, "You can do this, Coco. Come on, get up."

I sat back, resting my butt on the back of my legs with my hands fixed on the ground, I slipped my right leg forward and bent my knee to ninety degrees. With that foot planted, I scooched my left leg up. As soon as I stood blood rushed from my head, which made the trees dance and swirl like ballerinas. I toppled. I covered my face with my hands and rolled down the near side of the ditch into the cold stagnant water lining the bottom. My lips turned blue as carbon paper and my fingers became numb.

"Can't stay, can't stay here," played like a snare drum inside my head. In spite of cramping muscles, I clawed up the far side of the ditch and knelt exhausted on the hard edge of the road. I pushed myself up again and staggered to its center only to fall onto the rough rock. I curled my body into a ball like a baby blanketed in its mother's womb.

Time evaporated.

The sound of spinning stone made my eyes flick open. A car was barreling down the middle of the lane right toward me.

"Oh, he can't see me," I thought.

The car's tires skidded to an abrupt stop and I heard the stick shift thump. Both doors popped open. Shoes slapped against loose stone. Daddy scooped me up and cradled me in his arms. "It's okay, Coco. We'll get Mom."

"Curt, get the hell back into the car!" Daddy yelled at my twin brother as he ran with me in his arms toward the driver's door. After he slipped me into the middle of the Chevy's bench seat and got behind the wheel, I nestled into his warm chest.

The car doors slammed shut.

Daddy looked over his shoulder, put the car into reverse, and yanked the steering wheel hard to make a U-turn for home.

"A-h-e-r," I croaked.

Leaning his ear close to my mouth, Daddy said, "What? What do you need, honey?"

"W-a-h-e-r."

"Curt, when we get home I want you to go into the house and get your sister a glass of water. Okay?"

"Yup," Curt said, his eyes open wide like kernels of popped corn. Daddy raced up our driveway, blasting the horn. The garage door was open so he drove straight inside. I smelled pork chops frying.

Curt jumped from the car, ran up the three cement steps, and opened the kitchen screen door while I rested on Daddy's chest. Mom, still dressed in her morning housecoat, appeared in the open doorway holding a spatula in her right hand. She disappeared and within a minute was sitting beside me fully dressed as Curt passed a purple aluminum tumbler filled with water through the passenger side window. Grabbing the cool glass to my blistered lips, I tried to gulp the water down but Mom pulled it away from me after just one swallow.

"More," I begged.

"Just one sip, Carol," she said "or you'll get sick and throw up."

I pawed at the glass until she let me have another drink.

2

My father was a tender man: I was a daddy's girl. After working hard all day in the hog-kill, he liked to nap on our nubby, forest green couch. A scroll design, carved deep into the strong fabric of that sofa, made my skin itch when I sat bare-legged at its foot to untie Daddy's Red Wing work boots, which were fastened with round leather laces. The bow always slipped right open, but undoing the knot took a long time. I loosened the tight laces, removing them one row at a time, before grabbing the heel of his boot with both hands. Putting my full body weight into this task, I tugged hard. The boots were stubborn: they never released on either the first or the second try. As soon as a pop signaled release, Daddy wiggled his toes and then sighed. Zigzags of brown sweat marks, created by the friction between the shoe leather and his worn white cotton work socks, were a visible testament to his manual labor. After I removed his wet, smelly socks I covered him with a hand-crocheted afghan made by Grandma.

For the first seven years of my life my family lived on the east side of town in a cramped four-plex my Dad purchased with his VA benefit, having served in the Pacific Arena during WWII. All four of us kids, Teddy Bob, Scotty, Curt and me, spent our early childhood on South Railway, which got its name by being located just south of the Soo

Line Rail. Austin, Minnesota, was a working class town with a population just under thirty thousand where most everybody, including my dad, worked at Hormel, the local slaughterhouse and the home of SPAM. Daddy's steady pay-check was enough to plant our family squarely in the middle class. We would never know hunger. Indeed, we had steak at least once a week, pot roast on Sundays, and we were rich enough to occasionally go out for ribs at Lansing Corners, Mom's favorite restaurant.

It was a simple time. Even though we could not be mistaken for the families portrayed on TV, my family mirrored the hopes and dreams of the nineteen fifties. Dad worked, Mom cooked, and we kids (except for Scotty, my severely retarded brother) did well in school and kept our noses clean. Our phone, a party line, had only four digits. Mom purchased white lace Priscilla curtains from JC Penney's and picked an exuberant wallpaper pattern, featuring a cornucopia of fist-sized, deep-pink cabbage roses erupting across a pitch black backdrop, for the living room. After my twin brother and I were born, my parents shoved their double bed against one wall of their small bedroom in order to line up our cribs, end-to-end, on the opposite side. Teddy Bob shared the converted front porch with Scotty. Its walls and ceiling were constructed with slats of knotty pine slavered with knotholes tinted the deep cast of over-brewed coffee.

It took less than five minutes for us neighborhood kids to get from our house on South Railway to the train tracks. An old-fashioned milk processing dairy, constructed from red bricks, sat right next to the tracks. I remember it because of the full-sized Jersey cow on its roof. The cow made for good target practice: a licorice scorch mark, residue of a homemade cherry bomb resting just above her dangling pink udders, dared us to compete. Most times, Claude Angus, everyone called Sandy for obvious reasons, and his younger brother, Douglas, came along with Curt and me. Gathering pebbles from the track bed, we battled to see who could land the best hit. I never even came close to clobbering ol' Bessie, but then, being a girl, I was not expected to. When one of the boys' pebbles nailed the target, we all raised our arms and yelled out 'Banzai' in unison.

South Railway's front entrance opened to a foyer where six metal coat hooks lined up in military precision on either side. To the right and the left of the foyer, heavy wooden doors stood like sentinels and straight ahead, parallel with the street entrance, a big wooden staircase split the house. Once, when one of the upstairs apartments was vacant, my big brother, Teddy Bob, escorted me up the wooden staircase. I walked with trepidation across its cracked linoleum kitchen floors. Teddy grabbed my tiny hand as he pushed open the flimsy screen door leading to the open air porch, which spanned the entire front of the house. Loosening his grip, I ran to the rickety railing. The spring breeze licked my face. I could see all the way to the two-lane highway, adjacent to the hill containing the empty Soo Line train tracks. I was on the top of the world and I just knew it all belonged to me.

In the summer of 1957, Daddy took us all for a Sunday drive. We drove clear across town, past Sterling shopping center and the fairgrounds, to reach a residential development called the Acres. After traveling over three miles of uneven tar, we turned onto loose gravel and a quarter of a mile later Dad drove his 1947 olive Plymouth up a rutted path.

"This is it!" Daddy proudly proclaimed as he parked the car in a roughed-out driveway that led to an unfinished, ordinary, one-level house situated on a large lot. With three bedrooms and a big bath, my folks felt this modern house was a step-up; a better place to raise their family. They looked forward to swapping the stress of city life with plenty of fresh country air. No Peterbilt semi-trucks or train whistles split the silence in the Acres. The only sound was the crunch of an occasional car passing over the gravel. Teddy Bob hopped out of the back seat to open Mom's car door. Racing ahead of us all, Curt bounded into the attached garage, jumped up on the wooden plank (soon to be replaced with three cement steps) and disappeared into the house through the side door. Even then none of us headed for the front entrance, which would only be used by visitors in the coming years. Dad paced in a circle inside the two-car garage with a decided zip to his step. Turning, he motioned for Mom and me to hurry up. When Mom reached the side doorway, Dad extended his hand to help her step into what would eventually become our eat-in kitchen.

"Thanks, Ted," she said, as her eyes swept around the room. A shy eight-year-old girl, I nervously brought up the rear. Peering around, I couldn't imagine living here. It was barren: open studs, plywood sub-floors, and gaping holes waiting for windows. South Railway had charm and a sense of history. This house felt hollow to me.

"Finally a modern kitchen," Mom sighed, while staring wistfully out an open window frame into the backyard. She relished having a window over the sink—no more staring at a blank wall. She was finished with the one-banger, chipped, white porcelain sink and its attached ribbed drain board. For this modern house, she had ordered a divided stainless steel sink. Motioning me to her side, she put her arm around my shoulder, and while hugging me said, "Look, your room will be right here next to the kitchen."

Kicking my left foot back and forth, I nestled into her soft chest. My future bedroom had two doorways, one off the kitchen and the other off the hallway that transected the bedrooms and the bath. I would have a straight shot into the bath, giving me a clear advantage over my brothers. And there was a double closet, unlike the knotty pine porch (which had none), that had become my very own space two years before. With the exception of the basement laundry, this house had everything on one level. Curt and I would never again get the chance to dodge the water balloons Teddy Bob tried to drop on our heads from the second floor porch, and if we wanted to play hide-and-seek, it would have to happen outside. Four times the size of South Railway's, our new deep backyard was barren except for a mammoth propane holding tank and one lonely crab apple tree. I already missed the alleys and sidewalks of city life.

Our move took place in late September. Now that we lived so far out of town we had to take a yellow school bus to get to school. Like the new house, Banfield Elementary, was also modern, having been built two years before to accommodate Austin's burgeoning population. Since it housed two third grade classrooms, my twin brother and I were separated for the very first time. Curt didn't care a whit, but I felt alone and depressed.

After we moved, my grandfather, a house painter by trade used a trowel to plaster inch-deep, three-quarter swirls across the living room ceiling. Mom's nubby, dark brown reading chair and foot stool sat in the corner closest to the kitchen and Dad's turquoise Naugahyde La-Z-Boy, the biggest chair in the house, was placed next to the big picture window. By then we owned a television set. Our primary evening activity centered around that Philco. As a family, we passed the popcorn bowl or ate heaping bowls, not just a scoop, of ice cream while watching The Ed Sullivan Show, Father Knows Best, The Adventures of Ozzie and Harriet, I Love Lucy and my personal favorite, The Alfred Hitchcock Hour.

His family lived in the Acres too, high above Turtle Creek on a wooded lot a few miles from our house. Unlike our modest tract-house, their multi-level house, topped with a flat roof, looked chic and ultra-modern.

David James Torgerson was born on July 13, 1943, fourteen months after the birth of his oldest sister. Another boy, Wayne, came along three years later. When David turned twelve his mother gave birth to a second girl and, the final baby of their family, another girl, was born three years after that. I never knew anyone from their family but Curt knew his brother, Wayne, although they never hung out together.

Some of Torgerson's neighbors may have known that their son, David, had a police record by his tenth birthday but I did not hear of his attempts to grab little girls until my first Girl Scout Troop meeting. He was sixteen then and nurtured desires more twisted than a bag of pretzels.

3

I named only one doll in my girlhood: I called her Cheryl. A gift from my favorite uncle, she arrived on my eighth birthday wearing an elegant blue organza dress. Her thick curly brown hair was covered with a gossamer hair net. Her hazel glass eyes, framed with thick black lashes, even blinked. I kept her in pristine condition. When I made my bed, I placed her, just so, on top of my pillow. Although my mother thought it silly, the next summer I insisted on taking Cheryl along on the family vacation to Joe's Lodge, a typical north woods resort outfitted with a dozen furnished log cabins on the shore of one of Minnesota's 10,000 lakes. At Joe's resort, three piers, each with four bass fishing boats attached, jutted out into the lake's not-so-clear blue water. Our cabin's main room, which featured a brick fireplace, served as kitchen, dining, and living space. The three bedroom's interior log walls did not reach all the way up to the ceiling. Red gingham curtains closed off each doorway.

On our way to the north woods, we stopped in Hackensack to eat lunch at a rustic restaurant where meals were served family style. We passed bowls of mashed potatoes, corn, and a platter of roast beef around the table, just like at home. After lunch, we walked over to the town square to see the ten foot cement statute of Paul Bunyan's fiancée, Lucette. Paul Bunyan, a larger-than-life American folk hero, embodied frontier vitality. He was a symbol of might just like my daddy. In my eyes, they were both willing to work hard and able to overcome all obstacles.

Dad drove the remaining three hours to the lake and then we all pitched in to unpack the car. Realizing my doll was missing, my chest heaved as I ran into the kitchen.

"I can't find Cheryl!" I bellowed.

"Go look in the back seat," Mom said, while continuing to empty the contents of the Coleman ice chest into the cabin's old fridge. "She is probably there".

I searched the entire car. I even looked under the front seat in case she had been pushed out of sight.

"She's not there. I must have left her in Hackensack!" I hiccupped, with a full stream of hot tears tumbling down my cheeks.

"You have other dolls, Carol," Mom said. "Just think, a poor little girl, who may have never even owned a doll before, probably found her."

Horrors.

I imagined Cheryl dragged in the dirt behind a dark-eyed girl who didn't even know how to look after her. I pictured her fancy blue dress faded and in tatters. Her perfectly coiffed hair was gone with the wind: only tufts of loose strands, standing stick-straight in patches around her mostly bald head, remained. I believed my treasured doll would become unkempt and unloved.

Taking one look at my crumpled face, Daddy said, "Lois, cook my steak when I get back."

My bare feet slapped across the cold floor as I ran to greet him when he walked through the cabin door around midnight. "Did you find her?" I asked.

"No, Coco, I'm sorry," he said, sighing as he pulled me into his lap. I burrowed my head into his shoulder, which supported the full weight of my loss. None of us knew then that the following summer I would become as lost as my special doll.

The next day, Daddy took us all fishing in the boat that came with the cabin rental. Since neither Mom nor I were about to bait a hook, we each took along a book to read. Wearing a plaid bathing suit, I stretched out on the boat's narrow front bench and watched the clumps of clouds hanging above me. I had just closed my eyes when light rain drops tickled my forearms. The blue sky turned purple. Waves began to push our small boat about as blustery wind shot across the water. Dad and Curt reeled in their lines. After Daddy pulled anchor, he revved the Evinrude and headed hell-bent for shore. I shivered as steady rain pelted my bare skin. Motioning Teddy to take the throttle, Dad stood tall and removed his shirt. Then he handed it to Mom, signaling her to pass it on. She rolled her eyes upward and shook her head from side-to-side: all my life she had told me Daddy would give me the shirt off his back. Now he had finally done it.

4

In the spring of 1959, my mom came up with a plan to help me become more social. I was reading a book in my bedroom but the sliding door between the kitchen and my room was open. I overheard her talking on the phone with her sister, my Aunt Shirley.

"Saw an ad in the Herald for the Girl Scouts. A new troop's forming over in the Heights," Mom said, while taking a long puff on her menthol cigarette. "I'm gonna sign Carol up. She's so shy. Thought it would get better after we moved. Split her and Curt up at school. Still depends on him too much and on me too."

Mom rattled the newspaper. "Listen to this, Shirl:

Just 4 Girls

> Let the Girl Scouts introduce your daughter to fun activities. She will make friends, acquire skills, earn merit badges, and can attend a week of camp with her troop the first week in August. Scouting helps girls grow strong.

"It's justa' small membership fee. I'm gonna call. It'll be good for her. Summer camp too."

Before busying herself making dinner, Mom cut out the application from the paper, wrote out a nine-dollar check, addressed and sealed the envelope, and then called for me to run it out to the mailbox.

Lucky me.

This was the perfect plan—unlike the tap dance fiasco when I was five. Like many moms, mine imagined me at my first dance recital all dressed up in a cute little outfit: black patent-leather shoes, white socks with lace edges, and a red and white polka dot dress with a hint of scarlet crinoline underneath. She pictured me tapping away to the rhythm of the beat. I would be the star and she would be the envy of the other mothers. Her plans failed when I couldn't remember even one dance step from the first lesson, and then she realized she would have to learn all of the dance steps too. That was the end of it: we became drop-outs before the second lesson.

But the Girl Scouts would be different. All Mom had to do was pay a small fee, drive me to the meetings, and come back three hours later to pick me up. She made sure I had everything I needed, including that putrid green Girl Scout uniform which, knowing I would outgrow it in one season, she bought at the second-hand store. Mom and I drove in silence all the way across town to the Heights for the first den meeting.

The Foster residence, a two-story Georgian brick house, was a cut above ours. Amber light, highlighting attached window planter boxes filled with red geraniums, flooded their front walkway. After ringing the doorbell, we entered the front room, filled to the brim with young girls. A floral couch, framed by lace curtains, was placed beneath the picture window. Matching maple end tables, adorned with coordinating biscuit colored lamps, accented the sofa.

Mrs. Foster, the leader of troop 197, greeted us. "I'm so glad you came and that you remembered to wear your uniform," she said while patting the top of my head. She was the perfect fifties woman: Loretta Young, June Cleaver, and Betty Crocker, all rolled up into one. Her perfectly applied lipstick gave her mouth just the right definition and her pink shirtwaist dress accentuated her svelte figure.

"Let's step into the kitchen for a moment, all right?" I stood in the corner waiting to be told what to do. "Tonight we're going to take Carol's picture and she will make her very own picture frame for it. I know it will become a treasure you will want to keep forever," Mrs. Foster said to my mom adding, "You are more than welcome to stay and help out." Mom politely declined and, after urging me to have a good time, escaped out the side door.

Mrs. Foster poked her head out the arched cove, which connected the dining room with the kitchen, and called out, "Diane, come in here. I want you to meet Carol." Diane, who had been giggling conspiratorially with the other girls in the living room, sidled into the kitchen. Her cropped red hair matched the freckles that coated her face and arms. Presenting an impatient face, she motioned for me to follow her into the living room where a dozen girls had gathered.

As we passed through the dining room, I caught a glimpse of the formal dining table covered with supplies for the night's activity. A plastic ice cream pail holding hundreds of Popsicle sticks anchored the middle. Elmer's glue bottles, along with vials of red, white and blue glitter, laid scattered around the table. Barbara, who sat just outside the perimeter of the circle, flashed me a hopeful eager smile—her welcoming wide grin exposed an overbite with crossed front teeth. Barbara's dark brown, wide-set eyes nestled below a broad forehead. Her face looked flattened. Waving her short arms, she gestured for me to sit near her. From her perch on a footstool, her toes, dangling at the end of her noticeably bowed legs, barely brushed the gold shag carpet.

This was the first time I had seen a midget in real life. I settled on the soft rug and tuned into the gossip swirling around the circle.

"Yah, and this guy David grabbed Mary Peterson's little sister by the hand and tried to pull her out of the yard," an agitated girl named Nicloe announced. "But then her mom come running out and took her back."

Tension ruffled around the circle.

"My mom says he's a retard. That's why," Barbara confided.

My face colored like a bright pink sunrise. Indignation ignited me. I felt heat rise through my chest and flick up my neck like the flames of a bonfire. "That's not fair!" I said in a taut voice. "I have a retarded brother and he doesn't do those things."

A pale uneasiness engulfed the circle.

"Well, David lives in the Acres just like we do, so you better watch out," Nicole retorted, staring directly into my eyes. "That's all."

Mrs. Foster joined the group and a hush settled over our troop as she raised her right hand. One-by-one, the girls in the circle mimicked her gesture.

"Scouts, I'm so glad you remembered the quiet sign," she exclaimed. "Now, let's all hold hands! Left palm up, right palm down, close your eyes and settle your mind." After a few moments of silence, she whispered, "Give each other a friendship squeeze and gently open your eyes. Letting her eyes travel around the circle, she said, "Welcome each other with a big smile—eyes and mouth too!"

Disdain slid across my face. I was never good at hiding my feelings but it didn't matter much since Mrs. Foster wasn't discerning like my mom. Standing, she ushered us into the dining room where she showed us how to construct a picture frame from Popsicle sticks.

While we girls worked on our picture frames she called us one by one into the living room to pose for the soon-to-be-cherished Kodak moment. Posing patiently, I folded my hands in my lap as Mrs. Foster's camera whirred away. Docile as a mannequin on display in Woolworth's front window, I felt awkward in that ugly gabardine Girl Scout uniform—ironed and starched with care by my mom the night before. The waist fit tight and the skirt drew attention to my girl hips and knobby knees. Because my thick hair was riddled with cowlicks, I needed lots of bobby pins to hold the Girl Scout beanie that Mrs. Foster plopped at an angle on my head. Even though often unmanageable, I was vain about my hair, which fell like a platinum waterfall onto my shoulders. It was the one wild and free aspect of my existence. Of all the scouts who had their photos taken that day, I smiled the least.

Around 9:00 p.m., mothers returned to pick up their respective daughters. The evening concluded with refreshments: homemade cutout cookies, decorated by Mrs. Foster's very own capable hands, pink punch, which we scouts were careful not to spill, and coffee for the adults.

5

The night before my attack, I woke my mother from a sound sleep with my screams. At ten-years-old, this was the first nightmare of my life, at least one bold enough to make me cry out in my sleep. The clock signaled 3:00 a.m. Mom slipped on her nightgown, dashed the five diagonal feet separating our bedrooms and flipped my light switch. I felt the bed give way as she perched on the edge of my twin bed. I sat up with my eyes still closed tight and open mouth howling. As soon as she put her arms around me, I clutched Mom's neck and thrust my cheek into her boobs.

"Carol, what's the matter?" Mom asked, brushing my damp hair away from my face.

"They're coming to get me. They're going to get me," I sobbed.

"Who, who?"

"The elephants and the giraffes."

"Elephants and giraffes?"

"Yes," I wailed. "Stomping toward me, making big clouds of dust."

"It's Okay, it's Okay. Shush, shush now," she soothed. "You're having a nightmare. Look, look around—no elephants, no giraffes. You must have had too much candy before you went to bed," she admonished before instructing, "Calm down now and go back to sleep. You are safe in your room. It's just a bad dream. Everything is Okay. Nothing bad is going to happen."

Waking the next morning after fitful sleep, I stretched, and then threw my bare legs to the side of the bed. I put on a red polka dot tube top, white cotton underpants, red shorts, and white sandals. While sitting with my mother at the kitchen table, I twirled my fork in leftover syrup from the pancake breakfast.

"Mom, can I go on a picnic?" I asked.

Surprised, she set down her coffee cup and with arched eyebrows peered over the morning paper. She couldn't believe her ears. Most of the time she had to coax and cajole me to put down my books and go outside to play.

"Where would you go?" she asked.

"To the woods, Turtle creek, near the Wright house."

Mom stood to refill her coffee cup from the pot on the stove. Walking to the doorway, she looked into the living room and said, "Curtis, your sister wants to go on a picnic. I want you to go with her."

Turning from watching *Tom and Jerry*, my twin brother obliged her with a nod of his head. While he changed out of his p.j.'s I watched her make peanut butter sandwiches for our picnic lunch. Pulling out two brown bags from the cupboard, she placed a sandwich and an apple in each one. She put a Hostess chocolate cupcake into one sack, which was meant for me, and a banana flip, Curt's favorite, into the other one. Curt and I walked down our driveway, turned right, and rounded the first point of the triangle—a patch of grass situated across the road from our house marked at each point with a pine tree. Sometimes we neighborhood kids gathered there to play kick the can or a pick-up game of softball. Hitting a homer was easier on a half-diamond.

In less than a minute, we were out of Mom's eyesight. Our pace slowed when we reached Dvebeck's yard. Jimmy and his older brother, Charles, faced-off with other neighborhood boys in a rowdy game of football on their freshly mown turf. Their front lawn was almost as big as our back yard. From a pile of bodies, Jimmy called out, "Come on an' play!"

"Naw, I can't. I hafta take my sister on a picnic," Curt said, as he scuffed the tip of his tennis shoe in the dirt road.

"She can play, too!" a chorus of voices responded.

Curt turned to me with a pleading, eager face.

"You go ahead," I told him. No way was I gonna play football with a bunch of boys.

He hesitated.

"You can stay. I'll go on by myself," I insisted. "Go. I'll be fine. Go."

Without a backward glance, Curt darted into the middle of the huddle joining the neighborhood gang while I headed off on my own. I planned to picnic beneath the biggest tree in the Acres—a sturdy century old oak, surrounded with tall grasses. The school bus passed it while delivering the privileged few kids who lived near the woods above Turtle Creek. It seemed like a romantic place to have my picnic.

I heard Curt yell out, "Hut one, two, three," as I sauntered up the twisting gravel road. Boy grunts, groans, and victory yelps receded by the time I reached the Langowski house, a yellow Cape-cod with chocolate shutters. A Virgin Mary, planted in their side yard, sat tipped slightly to the right. The four Langowski boys attended Pacelli, the town's Catholic high school, so they never rode on the school bus with the rest of us.

I saw Carl, the oldest boy, bent over working in their yard. He was wearing ugly reflective orange shorts. I figured his mother probably bought them at the Goodwill and felt sorry for him because he had to wear such dorky clothes. I really liked Mrs. Langowski though. Every Halloween she cooked up a mountain of buttery popcorn balls. Each time I rang her doorbell, she would say with a smile, "I saved these two just for you, Carol." Maybe she treated me special because she didn't have a daughter of her own—I didn't know and didn't care, I was just glad to get the extra popcorn ball. Sometimes, when she ran errands, I rode along in their rusty station wagon. Strolling past their house now reminded me of the last time I did that. I don't know where we went or what we bought but I sure do remember what happened.

While driving the car down Austin's Main Street, Mrs. Langowski announced, "Four o'clock, boys!" Without hesitation, all four boys dropped to their knees on the floorboard of the wagon's backseat, each one of them pulled a chain of pretty beads from their pockets, and started to mutter a mysterious chant. I swiveled my head around and stared.

Seeing my surprise, Mrs. Langowski explained in a conspiratorial voice, "Carol, dear, in order to get to heaven, all good Catholics must say the rosary at least four times a day." When I got home, I told mom all about it. And then she told me not to ride with them anymore.

Walking further down the road, my mind turned to girlish thoughts about a boy who caught my eye late last spring. Although we rode the same school bus to Banfield Elementary for the past two years, we never said a word to each other. Most likely, he never even noticed me. Still, whenever I caught a glimpse of him before school let out for summer break, my heart beat faster. How could I have not noticed him before? I liked to daydream about his black

Brylcreamed hair and Gypsy Valentino eyes. Foolishly, I hoped he'd be sitting under the big oak tree when I got there. Time passes quickly when you are a young girl lost in the reveries of a first crush. I reached the isolated gravel road that twists and turns along the woods above Turtle Creek without even knowing it, but then two huge black birds swooped down from the sky. Their cries unsettled me. I stopped, opened my brown paper bag, and pulled out the apple mom packed for my picnic lunch.

Standing still in the road, I bit into it. Sweet juice trickled down my chin. After I finished with the apple, I wiped my mouth with the back of my hand, which is when the screeching crows returned. They circled and dived, blocking my way, increasing my uneasiness. To distract them, I threw the apple core into the ditch on the side of the road. That's when I saw him. He stood a few feet back from the edge of the woods. His dark-rimmed glasses, blue jeans, white tee shirt, white socks, and loafers made him look like a scrawny teenage Buddy Holly wannabe. His face was cast in shadow. Dappled sunlight accentuated his outstretched hands.

He said, "Can you help me? I need to find Sunnyside Avenue."

"You must be lost," I replied, real polite, like I had been taught by my mom. "There are no street names here. Just route one, route two, or three."

He took three steps back, turned toward Turtle Creek, which curved along the back of the woods, and disappeared back into the trees.

6

Just like on every other day, Mom opened the refrigerator considering what to fix for supper— maybe baked chicken? No, too hot to turn on the oven. Pork chops. Yeah, fry some pork chops and potatoes. Cut up a salad. Ice cream for desert.

My body plunges into darkness.

Mom filled a four-quart pot and set it to boil on the gas stove.

I wake. I want my twin bed with its iron headboard and the ballerina cerulean bedspread.

Taking a five pound bag of potatoes from the cupboard, Mom dumped a handful of spuds into the sink, ran them under the tap, and then scrubbed them clean.

I moan.

She plopped the potatoes into the boiling water and set the timer for twenty minutes. Time enough to read the newspaper.

My eyes slit open. My hands flit across my sunburned face.

The kitchen stove's timer dinged. After draining the hot liquid, Mom placed the cooked potatoes to cool in the refrigerator, took out the plastic bag of left-over ironing, and carried it into the basement. Fifteen degrees cooler, the basement was a better place to work.

Gnats, chiggers, and persistent mosquitoes dart around my puffy face.

Mom licked her index finger and touched the iron, testing to see whether it was hot enough. She placed a pillow case on the ironing board and pressed the wrinkles out.

A barbed wire fence cradles my sagging body. Sharp stings travel up and down my bare legs.

After folding the pillow cover in half twice, until it formed a perfect square, she pushed the iron across the top of the pillow slip one more time. As soon as five cases were piled neatly together, she unplugged the iron, carried the bundle upstairs, and put them away in the linen closet.

The sun hangs low in the sky. No one is going to find me.

Ted will be home from work soon, Mom thought to herself. Better set the table. A little after 5 p.m., the garage door whirled open. Mom heard the car door bang shut just before Dad stepped into to kitchen. He gave her a peck on the cheek.

My knees give way. I drop. My head and chest flop: Raggedy Ann—no Andy.

"Where're the kids?" Dad asked, sitting at the black Formica kitchen table to unlace his Red Wing boots.

"Teddy Bob left 'bout an hour ago to visit Gary Hanson. He should be home soon," Mom said, while grabbing the bowl of potatoes from the fridge and a paring knife from the drawer. She joined him at the table.

"What about the twins?"

"Gosh, I haven't seen them all day. I packed 'em a picnic lunch this morning. They should come rolling in anytime now."

Dad carried his boots into the back bedroom and took off his work shirt. Returning to the kitchen in his white undershirt, he opened the refrigerator looking for a cold beer to take the bite out of this hot July day.

I crawl in the dirt.

"I'm starved! When's dinner?" Curt said, as he vaulted through the side door to the kitchen.

"Six o'clock. Just like every night," Mom replied. "Where's your sister?"

"Don't know."

The sky has deepened like a fresh bruise. I see the road.

"Where did she go after the picnic?"

"Ah, I dunno."

"Huh? Whaddya mean?" Dad said.

"I didn't go with her. The Debvek boys were playing football. She said, 'Go ahead' so I did. Fran made us lunch. Then me and Jimmy worked on the fort out in their backyard."

There's a ditch.

"Where was she headed?" Dad asked Mom while taking a big gulp of beer.

I stand.

"Up to the creek by Susie Wright's. She's probably over there. Why don't you go pick her up, Ted. I'll hold supper 'til you get back."

The trees sway.

"Yeah, Okay," Dad said, placing the bottle on the kitchen counter. He got his black shoes out of the bedroom closet and slipped them on in the living room where Curt was watching TV.

"Curt, wanna ride along with me to pick up your sister?"

"Sure, Dad."

Hearing spinning stone, my eyes flick open.

7

The town hospital was about ten miles from our house. Dad made good time on the country back roads but when he turned onto Main Street, panic made his chest grow tight because three stoplights lay between us and the hospital.

"Lois, I am going to hit the horn and run them red lights!"

"No, Ted. She's all right," Mom snapped. "Don't get us in an accident. Just wait for the light."

I heard Daddy breathing hard as he waited for the green light. When we got to the hospital, he parked the car near the emergency entrance and ran inside to get help. Two guys in white coats came out with a gurney. They reached for me but Dad pushed them back. His touch was tender as he lifted me from the car and lay me on the crisp white sheets. The emergency doors flew open. The cart sped down the hall, stopped, and then turned into an empty examination room. After hustling me inside, more men in white coats appeared. "You have to stay out here!" one of them demanded, putting his hand on Daddy's chest. Another attendant yelled, "One, two, three." I was lifted from the gurney and placed onto a cold silver table in the middle of the room. My body jumped up and down. One guy grabbed a rolling stool and moved into position behind my head as more men in white coats raced through the double swinging doors converging all around me.

"Let's go!" one of them commanded. Descending from behind my head, a translucent gel cup covered my mouth and nose I tumbled back into nothingness. When I woke up, the room was filled with strange men dressed in either blue or white uniforms. Their tension was obvious—I could smell it as it cut across the antiseptic space.

"I am Lieutenant Anderson, Mr. Haack," I heard a police officer in the hallway say. Oh good, Daddy's still here, I consoled myself. "We've taken your daughter's belongings for evidence. There was only one white sandal. Do you have the other one?"

Dad must have shaken his head no because the policeman continued, "Okay, we'll search for it at the scene. You can get her clothes back after the investigation."

"We don't want them. You keep 'em," Mom said. "I'd just have to burn them."

"My detective tells me this happened in the Acres," he replied. "Is that right, Ma'am?"

"Yes. That's where we live."

"Don't worry," he said. "We have a pretty good idea who did this. I will dispatch a couple of officers out there to bring him in."

"How's she doing, doc?" the police lieutenant asked one of the doctors after coming back into the exam room. The doctor turned my head toward the blank wall. "See here: her jaw is swollen—we'll have to do x-rays. And these deep bruises around her throat…" the doctor moved his hand up and down the side of my neck. "Plus she has massive petechiae, burst blood vessels, not just her eyes, probably her lungs too—all classic signs of being strangled. Really, she should be dead," he said with a tight voice. "If he had held on for just one more second she wouldn't be here."

"Was she raped?" a burly cop asked, stepping forward.

The air was sucked out of the emergency room. My childhood innocence floated toward the harsh florescent lights, bursting in an instant like a soap bubble. Responding to the condemnation in his tone, I sat up fast. "No, no. I'm a good girl," I whimpered into the dead air, but no one seemed to notice me.

"No. He just tried to strangle her to death," the doctor paused, drew a breath. "It's a miracle, really. Like I said before, she should be dead."

With my virtue confirmed, I lay back flat on the table just before another white coat burst through the doorway. "Hello, Sergeant. I'm Doctor Peterson. Did David Torgerson do this?" he asked.

My head whirled. David! David, the creepy guy Diane and Barbara gossiped about at the Girl Scout meeting? The one Nicole warned me about?

"Looks like it, Doc."

"Oh, my God. I'm so sorry," he exclaimed, waving his clipboard near my face. "He tried to grab my four-year-old last weekend. I should have reported it," he confessed to the officer, clenching his free fist in the air as he shook his head back and forth in denial. "I talked with his folks. They said they'd take care of it! Oh, God," he exclaimed, before his chin dropped onto his chest.

"Don't feel too bad," the big cop told him. "We've had lots of reports on him, but our hands were tied 'cuz he's never hurt anyone before. Now, we can finally do something."

Everyone was so busy talking about what happened to me, they were oblivious to my body thumping up and down on the cold, impervious table. Feeling sick to my stomach, I sat up in a panic. My mouth ballooned and my cheeks filled up like a stuffed pocket gopher. A nurse, the only woman in the room, glanced in my direction.

"Do you need to throw-up, honey?"

I nodded my head. She grabbed a silver bedpan and spun around, maneuvering it just in time under my chin. Blood burst forth from my mouth like a small volcano. My eyes widened in disbelief as droplets splattered up the sides of the bowl.

"Water, I need more water," I croaked.

"Okay, here sweetie. I'll get you some ice chips to suck on," she said, placing feather pillows behind my neck and shoulders in order to prop me up. The cool melting chips met my blistered mouth. I had a moment of relief before another wave of nausea hit my guts and I began to choke.

"Doctor," the nurse implored.

"Oh, it's just the anesthesia," he said, his tone dismissive. "We put her under for the pelvic exam."

Then, as if playing from the same score card, all of the men, except for a lone orderly, left the room in unison. The attending nurse asked me if I was able to sit up long enough to ride in the wheel chair to my room. I shook my head yes. But I couldn't. My head drooped against my chest.

"Leo, let's put her back on the gurney," the nurse said.

Once we were outside the emergency room, we picked up Momma and Daddy. The hallway's shiny linoleum zipped by as we all hurried down the hall. After exiting the elevator at the third floor, I saw red, blue and yellow paper balloons decorating the walls. As soon as we entered room 302 on the children's ward, I screamed.

"Oh no. Elephants. Giraffes. Momma, the elephants and giraffes!" I kicked my feet and tried to sit up. "The same as last night. Coming to get me! Ohh," I pleaded, "make them go away!"

"It's Okay. Carol. They are just curtains," Mom said, trying to reason with me.

I reacted like a June bug stuck on its back by pulling my knees up and flailing my arms and legs about.

"What's the matter, Lois?" Daddy asked. "What's she afraid of?"

"It's the curtains, Ted," Mom said. "Get rid of them."

Marching to the window, Dad pulled the curtains, rod and all down, and then he balled them up and handed them off to the attending nurse. She hesitated for a moment before thrusting them into the hall—no one wants to mess with my daddy when he is angry.

When the orderly turned the gurney parallel with the single bed, I caught a glimpse of my bloated face in the mirrored wooden dresser sitting across from the bed. Floating under mats of vomit-filled hair plastered tight against my head, my eyes blazed like Kingsford red hot embers. Not one speck of white nor any hint of my once blue irises remained. Bold, blood-red orbs with pinpoint black dots of pupil stared back at me. I looked sub-human: grisly and grotesque. This can't be me, I thought to myself.

But it was.

I put my face in my hands and sobbed as the nurse grabbed a sheet from one of the bureau drawers to cover the mirror. Daddy pulled a wooden chair up to my bedside and patted my shoulder. "Daddy, Daddy. How did you know me?" I whimpered. "I am so ugly."

"You're my baby, Princess," he said, his eyes filling with tears. "I would know you anywhere."

I turned my head into the comfort of the down pillow as despair blanketed me.

"I don't think we can get a comb through her hair. It's too matted with vomit, debris, and dried blood," the nurse said in a stage whisper walking to the end of the bed where my mother stood. "What should we do?"

"Cut it. Cut it all off," Mom said curtly.

"Do you want to do it?" the nurse asked returning with a six-inch pair of scissors usually used to cut surgical packages open.

"No, you go ahead," Mom said, directing her chin in my direction. The nurse pushed the scissors through each nasty clump and disposed one after another into a green metal waste basket placed at my bedside. A couple of the globs escaped and fell onto the cold linoleum floor. My vanity vanished—forfeited along with my cascading curls.

> I heard car doors slam before the doorbell rang.

"David, come down here!" Harold Torgerson yelled up the stairs. "The police want to talk to you."'

8

Mom stayed with me throughout the first night. At 2:00 a.m. a nurse woke me up to give me something to make me sleep. The next day the doctor came in and checked my eyes. They still looked like the eyes of the devil. Every blood vessel had burst under the pressure of Torgerson's hard hands.

"Carol, you need to apply this salve into your eyes three times a day," the doctor instructed. "Just hold your eyelid open like this," he said using his thumb and forefinger to prop my eye open, "then push lightly on this tube, and draw a bead across your eyeball. See, it doesn't hurt," he told me while depositing a glob of salve along the lower rim. "Now, smooch your eyelids together."

I did what I was told.

"That's a good girl," he said, patting my arm before turning to Mom. "Her eyes will return to normal but, for the next month, make sure she wears dark sunglasses to protect them. She should also take it pretty easy. The assault caused her to bleed out through her ears, nose and mouth and made the blood vessels in her lungs explode. Her physical endurance will probably be compromised for a while. In a month or so we'll check them again along with her left ear drum."

Mom sat with me all through the first two days until Aunt Naomi, who is married to Herman, my dad's brother, came to relieve her on the second evening.

Herman and Naomi were deacons in the Church of Christ. They often took my cousin Priscilla and me to church along with their daughters Judy and Sharon. Naomi also sold Stanley cleaning products at house parties. In her house, shiny gold statues, displayed on three-tiered glass shelves backed by a beveled mirror, stood as a testament to her saleswomanship.

"You go on home now, Lois. I'll take good care of our girl," Naomi said, fussing with my blanket and sheets. "You need to get some rest too. Don't worry, we'll be just fine."

But I wasn't just fine. And on this night sleep did not visit me. I was so troubled Naomi pressed the little yellow button hanging from a cord above my bed. When the nurse appeared, she asked her to get something to calm me down so I could sleep.

"I'm sorry Mrs. Haack, I can't bring her anything because the doctor didn't order it," the nurse replied while looking at my chart. "Since we had to wake her up last night to give her a sedative, the doctored figured she wouldn't need anything tonight."

"But she does," Naomi responded. "She is very agitated. Can't you ask the doctor for something?"

"I'm sorry. He has gone home for the night," the nurse responded with a frown. "I'll bring her some warm milk. Maybe that will help."

Naomi did her best to reassure me. She slid the big padded chair right next to the head of my bed so she could hold my hand and stroke my face. Still, I remained too frightened and upset to sleep. Just as visiting hours were ending, a man and a woman poked their heads into the corner of the room. The man's navy suit coordinated with his wife's shirtwaist dress. He clutched a soft wool Fedora hat in his well-manicured hands. Her patent leather heels and the strand of pearls she wore around her neck gleamed under the florescent light of the hospital room. She held her black handbag close to her body. As soon as she noticed this fashionable couple, Naomi jumped up and scurried to the doorway.

"Oh, hello," Naomi said.

"We heard you were here and just wanted to stop by," the tall man said while fingering the edge of his hat. "We hope that is okay?"

"Oh, sure," Naomi said with a thin smile.

"How are you?" the woman murmured, nodding in my direction.

"She is having trouble sleeping tonight," Naomi said. Returning to my bedside she began stroking my forehead. "But she's a brave girl. She'll be just fine."

Leaving my bedside and walking towards this well-dressed couple she said, "Let's talk in the hall so we don't disturb her."

The woman bit her lower lip and gave me a backward glance as she backed out of the room. I heard the three of them talk softly in the hall. Based on their manners, I decided they must be people from the church who had stopped to chat with my Aunt Naomi because she was a very important lady there.

Years later, my twin brother told me he too met this refined, straight-laced couple. He remembered them with even more precise detail than I did. Right after leaving my hospital room, they drove directly to our house to offer their apologies to my folks. Curt wondered why well-dressed strangers would come to our door so late in the evening. He figured the man couldn't be a packinghouse worker like our Dad because he wore a blue button-down dress shirt with a navy striped tie and his dress slacks matched his black dress shoes, shining with polish. Most packing house workers wore blue jeans and steel-toed leather boots. The tall man's wife, in a Sunday-go-to-meeting silk navy blue dress, clutched her real leather handbag with both hands. Unlike our family, Curt told me, the man did all of the talking after they stepped inside.

"We just came from visiting your little girl at the hospital. We are so very sorry our David hurt her like that. We just wanted you to know how sorry…"

Dad sat up in his recliner but said nothing.

"You have a very sick boy," mom said, removing her reading glasses. "He needs lots of help."

The room filled with sad silence.

This was the only time our two families ever met face-to-face. I never saw this unfamiliar couple again, not even at the court house.

Two days later *The Austin Daily Herald* ran typical the news of the day. The paper highlighted a picture of three young girls splashing in a kiddy wading pool and ran an article featuring an Ohio family who were eager to be the first to creep from coast-to-coast on a tractor. Crammed in the bottom corner of page three was this brief entry:

Youth, 16, in Psychiatric Examination, to Remain in Jail

A youth, 16, at a preliminary proceeding in Juvenile Court Friday afternoon, was referred for psychiatric examination in connection with an

> attack on a girl, 10, Tuesday in Austin Acres. The girl was grabbed by the throat and thrown to the ground. A physician said she was in very critical condition for a short time after the attack. She recovered and Thursday was released from St. Olaf Hospital. The youth will be held in the county jail for about two weeks while under psychiatric examination.

When I got home from the hospital, my Aunt Jean and her daughter, Priscilla, were the first to drop by. They caught me wearing my standard outfit: p.j.'s along with a new pair of dark sunglasses. I sat curled into the corner of our turquoise sateen couch. They handed me a gift—a jeweled tin that held small treasures: some chocolates, a beaded necklace, pink nail polish, and a game of pick-up sticks. This was the first time I have ever received a gift for no reason. Jean left Priscilla with me in the living room and joined my mom for coffee in the kitchen.

"What happened to you?" my cousin asked while standing awkwardly by the couch.

"I went to the woods for a picnic and this guy asked me where Sunnyside Avenue was. I told him, 'You must be lost. There are no streets or avenues here.' Then he grabbed and strangled me."

"For no reason? Didja know him?"

"Nope."

"Huh—Are you Okay?"

"Yeah. I guess."

The next visitors were not so polite: professional questioners, who purported to be on my side. Mom answered the door and let them in after they introduced themselves as the lawyers for the state. Their formal suits, starched white shirts and striped ties showed they were important men.

These fresh-faced, young attorneys appeared to be very excited about my case—more than likely they had only dealt with petty crimes, DWI, and burglaries before now. This would be their first big indictment and they wanted to do well. Telling Mom they needed to ask me a few questions to get me ready for the trial, they took two of our kitchen table chairs and pulled them up close to the living room couch where I sat. Each of them opened his leather bound brief case and removed yellow legal pads along with fancy ink pens.

"Carol, do you know who we are?" one of them asked, gesturing at himself and his partner.

Cornered, I curled myself deeper into the curve of the sofa.

"We are the lawyers who are going to try the case against David Torgerson," he continued. "Do you know who he is?"

"Uh huh," I mumbled.

"Is he a friend of yours?"

"No-o-o-o!"

"You sure?" he asked with a quirked eyebrow.

"Yes."

"Okay, let's get started," he said, motioning for the other to begin taking notes. "How old are you?"

"Ten."

"Do you know the difference between the truth and a lie?"

"Yes."

"What is a lie?"

"When you make something up."

"So if you told us you were fourteen that would be a lie, right?"

"Yes."

"Have you ever told a lie?" he asked leaning forward.

"No."

"No? Are you sure? Maybe you lied to your mom once, huh?"

"No."

The one who is writing notes on the yellow legal pad looked up and said with a false grin, "Are you sure? Can't you think of one time when you didn't tell the truth? Come on now, you can tell us. We are on your side."

"I don't lie."

The first one butted back in, "Okay, fine. Let's talk about what happened a week ago. . ."

"Yeah, just tell us what you did that day," the smiley guy added.

"Okay. I told my mom I wanted to go on a picnic in the woods and…"

"Why did you want to do *that?*" the first one challenged me.

"I dunno…"

"Are you sure?" he said. "Maybe you were planning to meet someone or something…"

For a moment, I worried they somehow knew about my secret crush on the sixth grade boy from my school bus but then they asked me more about David and I repeated that I didn't know him.

"But at the beginning you said you knew who he was, remember?"

"I know his name now. But I don't know him."

"Okay, right. Just remember, all we want is the truth here."

"I just wanted to go on a picnic and sit under the big tree."

"Yeah, but you knew he lived near there, didn't you?" he said, inching his chair closer to the sofa.

"I didn't know him," I repeated. "I don't know where he lives."

"Did he think you were fourteen?" the other one cut in.

I inched my body into the couch corner and pulled my knees up to my chest, "I don't…"

"All right, let's go back to the beginning again," the lead questioner exhaled, his breath stinking of bitter coffee. "You told your mom you wanted to go on a picnic and then what?"

"She packed us a lunch."

"Who is us? You and a friend?"

"No, me and my twin brother. Curt was going with me."

"Oh, okay so your brother was going on the picnic too."

"Yah, and when we got to Debvek's he stayed to play football," I explained.

"How come? Wasn't he supposed to go on the picnic too?"

With each question their voices grew stronger—harder, more accusing.

"Well, the kids asked him to play and I said, 'Okay'."

"Okay, what?"

"Okay, he should stay and play," I answered with a hint of heat in my tone.

"Didn't you want him on the picnic? I mean was there a reason why you wanted to go alone?"

"He wanted to play. That's all."

"Then what?"

"I went up the road toward the woods. And when I got there some big black birds screeched scaring me so I decided to go home."

"Hmmn."

"And then David walked out of the woods and asked me where Sunnyside Avenue was."

"Had you met him before?"

"No, I told you," I said, exasperated.

"Then what happened?"

"His hands, he held out his hands when he talked to me. They were big. He had big hands. They reminded me of Scotty's. I told him he musta' been lost. And I walked on down the road. Then he…"

"Who's Scott?"

"Scott is my retarded son," Mom cut in from her chair in the corner of the living room. "He doesn't live with us now. How much longer is this going to take?"

"Not much longer, Ma'am," the lawyer replied nodding in her direction. "We just have to make sure she'll be ready to testify."

Turning back to me he asked, "Did he walk down the road with you?"

"No, he turned and went back into the woods."

"Okay. Then what happened?"

"He grabbed me from behind and told me I wouldn't get hurt if I didn't scream."

"Did you scream anyway?"

"No."

"Why not," the note taker asked without looking up. "Did you know him?"

"No, I already said… I couldn't… His hand was pushing on my jaw and my mouth. Then I passed out."

"Then what happened. What did he do next?"

"I don't know," I said. "Later, in the afternoon, I woke up a lot. I felt sick and I wanted to go home."

"And? Was David still there?"

"No, just me," I said turning my head into the couch pillows. "I was all alone."

"Were you scared?" he asked, with the first tender tone in the whole exchange.

"Uh huh."

"Then what did you do?"

"I crawled to the road. And then Daddy found me."

"All right, let's go through this one more time… Do you know the difference between the truth and a lie?"

After two hours, they finally stood up. The note taker replaced the top of his ball point pen, shoved the yellow pad back into the briefcase, and clamped it shut.

"She'll make a good witness, Mrs. Haack. We'll call to let you know when you are on the court docket. "

9

The sheriff arrived after breakfast. The jailer opened the cell door and they both stepped inside.

"Stand up, David," the sheriff commanded, towering over him by a good half a foot. "We got to put these chains on you to take you on down to the courthouse."

They bound his wrists and ankles and flanked him for the quick walk past the other dozen mostly quiet cells. Once outside, he blinked against the August sun. His shackled hands and feet made him stumble some. The Sheriff placed his big paw on top of his head and pushed down directing him into the back of the van, another caged space. The vehicle shifted to the left as the Sheriff plopped his beefy body behind the wheel. Removing his hat for the drive, Torgerson noticed sweat had started to form on the back of the Sheriff's bald head before he rolled down the driver side window. After setting the van in motion, a breeze pushed against the dead air that had built up inside.

Two blocks later his lawyer greeted him inside the back doorway. Together they moved across the polished granite floors, a dappled mosaic of beige and black dots highlighted with flecks of glinting amethyst. His lawyer's wing-tips smacked on the smooth stone as Torgerson shuffled beside him in his tennis shoes, hampered by the chains that locked his feet six inches apart. An echo made him look up when they were halfway down the massive hall.

We showed up at the big courthouse on Main Street at 9 a.m. on Monday, August 1st. The marble corridors, lined with sturdy wooden doors that had black lettering stenciled on their opaque windows, overwhelmed me. The only sound came from the whirling fans hanging from the mile high ceilings.

Dad and Mom flanked me as we walked toward the room where the preliminary hearing was going to be held. Feeling anxious and nervous, I stopped to get a drink from the white porcelain water fountain. I turned the metal faucet, bent my head, and drank the cold water. When I looked up, I saw him approach from the corner of my eye.

He wore a beige jumpsuit and looked slight in contrast to the two men who were escorting him. The one wearing a suit and tie carried a big brown leather briefcase. The other one wore a beige uniform, but it was different from David's jumpsuit; a shiny badge, common to officers of the court, shown on his chest. The three of them stopped and looked down the hall at us. My body shook. I grabbed my dad around the waist and hid my head in his chest.

The hallway dripped with humidity and tension.

Daddy took a step forward. I didn't budge an inch so the lower half of my body slid behind Daddy's hip.

> I saw her tremble just before she hid behind a big guy's hip. The man glared at me. "Guess that's her dad," I decided.

Two steps later his lawyer's arm motioned him to a stop. They turned, walked away, and then slid into a small room.

"She recognized you, David," his lawyer said. "You need to take the plea."

The court officer opened a heavy wooden door, and right after they disappeared inside, one of the lawyers who had questioned me at our house came out. He walked confidently up to us and said, "Carol, do you know who that was?"

I didn't respond.

"Wait here until I come to get you," he yelled back at us as he turned to walk back down the hall.

The Juvenile Court record showed Torgerson had attacked several young girls without provocation on four separate occasions in September, October, and November of 1958. As a result of these attacks, he was seen at the Mental Health Clinic in Austin and at the Mayo Clinic in December of 1958. Notes from this psychiatric record revealed, "David James Torgerson has a resentful attitude toward women and girls, which probably stems from the fact he was the second child, born one year after his sister, with a younger brother and two younger sisters for whom he had to baby sit."

Five minutes later our lawyer emerged with a huge smile on his face. "You won't have to testify," he said after walking up to the three of us. "His lawyer saw how you looked when you saw him. They have decided to plead."

"What will happen to him?" Mom asked.

"He's a juvenile, so we'll ask that he be committed to a state mental hospital so he can get the help he needs. I will ask the court to create a notification order if he should ever be released."

The 1959 official court record specified that while picking berries in the woods the defendant grabbed a ten year old girl, dragged her into a thicket, and choked her violently to unconsciousness. Her face was mottled and blue, and the physician, who cared for the girl, said she was almost dead.

Picking berries, such an innocent activity, one that belied premeditation.

The presiding Judge, Hugh Plunkett, was not sympathetic. On August 13, 1959, exactly one month since his sixteenth birthday, Mower County Court found David Torgerson to be a mentally ill person and ordered him to be committed to an institution for the care of the mentally ill. The court order concluded, "This is necessary for the welfare and protection of the patient and society, and the court further finds that the defendant is 'a danger to the public'."

Satisfied with the outcome, we left the marble halls of justice, walked out into the bright sunlight, hopped into our car, and drove directly over to Grandpa's. Grandpa Walter lived on the East Side in a modest two-bedroom bungalow with my grandmother, Irene. Having recently retired from working and living fulltime at the State Mental Hospital in St. Peter, Minnesota, they knew a little something about violent, crazy people. But that was not the reason for our visit.

Grandpa bred Boston Terriers, little feisty black-and-white shorthaired dogs, and his bitch has just delivered five puppies. Even though the puppies were still too young to leave their mother, I got the first pick of the litter. I chose a wee female, naming her Cookie. When I held her in my arms, her soft coat and gentle kisses comforted me. Mom told me she would be waiting for me after I get home from Girl Scout camp, which started on the following Monday.

I had never willingly spent a night away from home let alone a whole week—I didn't want to go but the trip was already been paid for.

10

By noon he was on his way to Rochester State Mental Hospital, which had been built on a five hundred acre farm. The site contained over a dozen buildings: an ornate Victorian filled with administrative offices, a dedicated laundry, separate engine and boiler houses, two male wards, one female ward, two geriatric wards, and eleven staff houses. The hospital was staffed by doctors from the Mayo Clinic.

"This is David James Torgerson," a man dressed in white, who had escorted him to intake services, said. "Here's his booking sheet, court commitment papers, and personal effects."

"Take a seat David," the admitting clerk said, bobbing her head at the chair across the desk from her. "I need to sort through your bagged belongings to see if you have any sharps or unsafe items. Okay?"

I nodded.

"You can't have this razor, it's a sharp. Joe will give it to the team over in Building C. You can use it when you want to shave but you'll have to be supervised. You can't have this belt back either," she explained.

They took his belongings and catalogued them. He didn't expect to get any of it back. They didn't finger print or take his picture again: it was already in the system. The jailer back in Austin said it would be permanent—his record. It was forwarded to the state Bureau of Criminal Apprehension and the FBI too.

    I'm a big shot.

"I need to check your mouth. Open wide now," the clerk instructed Joe while pushed his fingers through his hair searching for contraband. The clerk pressed a rubber marker across an inked pad and with a flick of her wrist slapped 'Admitted,' in fire engine red on the top page.

"Soon as I sign and date this you're good to go. Someone at 'C' will fill you in on the rules there. We hope that your stay with us is a helpful and productive one," she said, dismissing him without looking up.

Tunnels led from the main administrative building to each of the five inmate wards. When they reached 'C' ward, where he would be housed, Joe pulled out a mess of keys dangling from a chain attached to his belt and unlocked the glass door. After it clanged shut, they all stepped to the next door and Joe pressed a round blue buzzer.

They waited.

He heard a chair scrape before the next orderly appeared in the middle of the blank hallway. After unlocking the door from the inside, both orderly's pushed him down a gleaming corridor until they reached a door marked 'C 29'.

"You'll be in lock-down," the new guy said, "and subject to checks."

"What's that?"

"Checks are a routine part of life on this ward. Every hour a staff member checks in on you. We always knock first and say 'checks' before entering though."

"What about during the night when I'm sleeping?"

"Then too. Twenty-four hours a day. We won't wake you," he added. "We're just making sure you're alright."

Joe set David's nearly empty bag down on the bare floor and saw him slump in the plain wood chair that sat next to his lone twin bed. "Get settled in now. I'll let Dr. Tyce know you've arrived," the new guy said. "He'll stop by soon."

David heard the keys jangle: the lock clicked, and then the door snapped shut.

11

Even though David Torgerson was packed off for treatment at the Rochester State Mental Hospital, I struggled with night terrors. Flashbacks flipped across my dreamscape: unfiltered, disjointed, and fleeting like the brief light of fire-flies shivering in an August night. On the first Friday in August of 1959, Mom prepared my bag for Girl Scout camp. Being a practical woman, she never questioned whether or not this was a good idea. She had prepaid for this week of camp on the night of the first troop meeting way last June. The money was now non-refundable. She hoped I would have fun and make friends.

She packed my favorite candy, chocolate covered peanut M&M's, my new nightgown (purchased for the hospital stay), my hair brush, a brand new pink tooth brush, and Colgate toothpaste, a couple of books, and, of course, the salve the doctor had prescribed for my eyes. She closed the small suitcase and placed a pair of dark wraparound sunglasses on top. Meant to guard my eyes from the bright sunlight, these protective shades also shielded me from intrusive stares.

The Girl Scout Camp was located five miles outside of town. Around midday, we drove up its gravel roadway, straddled with sparse straw-colored grass. Looking around, I spied a fire pit in the middle of the camp's worn, front yard. Pine benches circled a pile of prepared logs for that evening's bonfire.

Dad parked the car and carried my suitcase up to the wooden screen door, which opened into the log cabin's large front room. A long, rustic wood dining table, able to seat up to twenty scouts, ran along the length of the front windows. A big white porcelain sink with an attached drain board stood on the far side of the room. Aside from the cooking stove, it was the only modern convenience in the wood-hewn cabin. Since there was no electricity, every day one of the troop leaders had to drive into town to load up the day's food supply along with dry ice for the ancient ice box.

Mrs. Foster, our den mother, and Miss Larson, the senior scout mistress, greeted us in the open front room. At six feet, Miss Larson commanded attention. Her salt and pepper tightly permed hair added to her regal bearing. A woman with considerable talent, who devoted her life to developing the town's future citizens, Miss Larson was born to lead and she knew it. When she sang in the First Baptist Church choir, her clear, crisp alto voice was almost always on key. Miss Larson understood if you live sensibly you will never become lost. She was a sensible woman who ate a sensible diet and wore sensible, laced shoes. Had she been a man, she could have been the principal of the Heights Elementary School instead of just its sixth grade teacher.

A portion of the front room, where Mrs. Foster and Miss Larson slept, was curtained off. At the rear of the main room, French doors closed off the scouts' sleeping quarters. Rows of twin beds straddled the middle of the room and lined the walls. As soon as Dad left, Miss Larson told me to put my bag on any empty bed. Happy to find an unoccupied, corner bed next to a window, I unpacked my books and hid my M&M's under the pillow before placing my suitcase beneath the cot.

Lying on top of the bedcovers, I flipped open one of my favorite books, *Little Women*. I admired Jo's pluck and Meg's steadfastness, but the character I really want to emulate most of all was Beth. I yearned to be as serene, gentle, kind, and self-effacing. But, truth be told, I knew I was most like Amy—the least likeable and most spoiled character in the book.

Later, Mrs. Foster called us to assemble in the outer room where she pointed out the rules of the camp, which were posted in big print on the wall right under the Girl Scout slogan:

Do a Good Turn Daily

Rule One: Make your bed
Rule Two: Participate in all scheduled activities
Rule three: Pick up after yourself
Rule Four: Do not litter
Rule Five: Be kind to Nature, don't pick the flowers or plants

Mrs. Foster raised her right hand to silence the chattering scouts before taking us on what she called, 'Our Walk with Nature'. I wished I could be back on my bed with Jo, Amy, Beth, and Meg instead of lining up with the girls of Troop 197. Exiting the cabin, I noticed the Girl Scout Motto, **Be Prepared**, stenciled above the door. As we tramped around the side of the cabin to follow a winding path, a flock of crows cawed, flapping their wings as they flew off above the tree tops. My heart and head pounded with each step we took into the shadowed woods.

The woods were no longer a place to picnic, a place of beauty or solace, like before. It stopped being a place of girlish dreams—I did not want to be stranded there. Feeling scared, I made sure I was in the middle of the troop. In less than three city blocks, our troop arrived at a small clearing where a lone outhouse had been placed. This was not a space where I wanted to pull down my pants, especially if I was there all by myself.

As my fellow scouts opened and closed the creaking door, the unmistakable odor of pee and poop wafted up from the two holes in the bare plank. Mrs. Foster patiently waited while we each took our turn. Each day after lunch the troop leaders lined us all up to march down to the outhouse in a group. As soon as we finished our business we all hiked back to the front of the cabin where Miss Larson lined us up in pairs.

"Carol, Barbara, I want you two to come with me," Mrs. Foster said. Touching my shoulder, she motioned for me to climb into the front seat of a rattle-weary tan 1955 station wagon. Miss Larson was sitting at the wheel. Barbara propelled herself head first under the dash board, turned and then hoisted her rump into the middle of the bench seat. I can't believe it. Having devil eyes didn't mean I couldn't walk. Why was I the only one out of all of the scouts to be stuck with Barbara and prim Miss Larson? Life was so unfair. In order to escape the mid-day heat, I flopped my head out the side window. Sweat formed on my forehead and under my arms. Barbara (who was plainly overjoyed to have me sitting next to her) incessantly prattled on about the upcoming week's highlights: roasting marshmallows around the campfire, water sports, craft activities, and earning merit badges. Finally, she wasn't the only one who stuck out, the one to be avoided with sideways glances. She was not the only one who got whispered about. Now, she had me—a frightened girl protected against the light by dark wraparound sunglasses.

Puffs of dust curled up as the rattling wagon crept up the road following Girl Scout troop 197. Miss Larson tried to draw me into their conversation, but I did not want to be a good scout. It seemed there was no actual destination on that hot August morning. The scouts just traipsed up, then down, the tiresome gravel road as if they were in Marine boot camp. It was a test of endurance. Even though I had no desire to trudge along up front with the others, I still resented being forced into the car. In fact, I wished I wasn't at camp period. I wouldn't have chosen this even without having been strangled and traumatized. But no one ever asked me what I wanted or needed. If they had, I would have told the truth just like I was prepared to do in court. I would have said I wished I had died that day in the woods. It would have been so much easier; easier, at least, for me.

On the first evening of camp when we were given free time after supper most of the other girls choose outside activities. Some went canoeing or swimming. I curled up in the corner of my bed to read and ate M&M's. When the light failed, I grabbed my red vinyl cushion and wandered outside to join with the other girl scouts who were already sitting around the campfire. Miss Larson blew on her pitch pipe leading us in a rousing chorus of Row, Row, Row Your Boat until Mrs. Foster appeared with a platter of marshmallows, graham crackers, and Hershey bars. We all rushed to grab a stick and lined up to make S'mores. I loved how the crisp night air mingled the smell of the campfire with the scent of burning sugar and chocolate until I realized I need to pee.

"I need to use the bathroom," I said to Diane as I wiggled on my red vinyl cushion. "Will you come with me?"

"Naah," she replied, "We all went before the bonfire. It's too spooky to go after dark."

I hurried into the cabin and pulled my bag out from under the bed to see if Mom had packed me a flashlight. No luck. In desperate shape, I walked to the side of the cabin and stared down the winding path that led to the secluded outhouse. Moonlight cast shadows in the trees. I scrunched my eyes and peered helplessly into the darkness. Out of nowhere panic closed my throat. My breath became shallow and quick and, even though the night was cool, beads of sweat formed across my forehead. Suddenly, it seemed as if he was here again: coming up behind me, wrapping his arm around my waist, putting his free hand over my mouth, and ordering, "Don't scream."

Alarms exploded inside my head. I went mute with fear. I knew I would not be able to walk the woods to use the outhouse. "You're Okay, you're Okay," I crooned as I curled my arms across my chest hugging myself tight. Returning to the campfire, I inched the vinyl cushion away from the fire's sunset embers. I sat my butt down and furtively lifted my left butt cheek up and off the side of the cushion. I looked around to make sure no one was watching and then I peed straight into the hard ground.

The campfire had totally died out by the time I ran back into the cabin. Slipping through the main room, I quickly moved toward the safety of my bed. The troop leaders were busy orchestrating the tooth brushing line-up so I had time to throw my cotton nightgown over my head. Then I slid my soiled panties and shorts off and kicked them under the bed to dry out. After we all went to bed and the dark of the night closed around me, I couldn't sleep. First, I worried I had identified the wrong guy. What if he was still out there lurking and waiting, hunting me once again. Next, I imagined him as a leader of a gang making me a target of retribution. I kept a fretful watch on the night sky as panic settled on my shoulders. When the clock chimed twice my body was gripped with a fierce urgency. I regretted taking that second glass of Kool Aid. I rocked back and forth significant pain before I made a straightforward decision to pee directly into the sheets. Even though the tension in my body dissipated, I still couldn't fall asleep. Flitting images of running in the forest flooded my brain. I ran fast—faster than a squirrel scampers up a tree. I turned into a sleek gazelle. Even without wings, I could fly easily above the tree tops. Nothing could catch me. I always sailed out of reach. As these fantasies unfolded my panic eased and I finally fell to sleep.

After lunch on the second day, I slipped off to the comfort of my bed. As soon as I sat down, I felt a crinkling beneath the blanket and sheets. My face burned crimson as any campfire when I discovered a rubber sheet had been placed on my bed and, just like in the hospital, I was infected with shame. Neither Mrs. Foster nor Miss Larson ever asked me about it. I suppose they were too uncomfortable to do more than murmur to each other, 'poor girl'. My mom must have told them what happened to me when she explained about my eyes. Otherwise, they would not have put me in that stupid car. All they had to do was take me to the outhouse before bed. But they never did.

Not only was there no indoor plumbing at summer camp, there were, of course, no mirrors. Not that I needed one to apply the salve to my eyes. I did that, even in the darkness of the night, by facing the wall, which kept anyone from seeing my eyes. Near the end of the week, I began to wonder if the medicine had made a change. I became curious to see what my eyes looked like. Sitting on my bed with sunshine sifting through the window, I could hear the clink of the utensils, the sizzle of bacon, and the faint whisper of hungry campers coming from the common room. Like me, several other girls had dawdled behind, not quite ready to start the day. I hesitantly approached the nearest one.

"Mary Ellen, do you have a mirror?"

"Whadaya need it for?" she retorted.

"Uhm... I want to check my eyes."

"Okay, but only if we get to see them too. Deal?"

Curiosity, coupled with a wanting to belong, overcame my instinct to remain private. A small collection of girls crowded on the bed next to mine. Then Mary Ellen, with all of the hush and ceremony of Sunday morning communion, passed me her hand mirror. The room grew quiet with expectation.

After a moment's hesitation, I raised my hand to remove the sunglasses that had been such an immutable fixture this whole week. Slowly, I lifted my gaze and looked directly into their expectant faces. My heart sank as they tumbled off the bed and scurried from the room howling like a pack of coyotes. I had not anticipated their horrified reaction. With dread and a trembling hand, I lifted the mirror from my lap, and then softly shuddered. Last week, when I looked in the mirror there had been only a blaze of solid red staring back at me. Now, there was a hint of iris, a faint shimmer of blue, and also visible in my left eye, two specks of white. They were beautiful. I thought my eyes looked beautiful. They had started to look like the eyes of a child again. After a moment's reflection, I groaned in anguish and relief. Although I would never see the world through the telescope of childhood innocence again, I had started to heal and to grow strong—just like the Girl Scouts promised.

When the last day of camp arrived, I was too excited and relieved to eat. I packed my bag way before breakfast and stood on the front porch waiting for Mom and Dad to drive up the gravel road. When they pulled up, I jumped into the back seat almost before the car came to a halt.

"How was camp?"

"Okay. I guess."

"Are you ready to go home? Isn't there anyone you want to say goodbye to?" Mom asked with a tinge of hope in her voice.

I considered saying goodbye to Barbara, the only other camper who knew more than I did what it feels like to be ostracized for something beyond your control, but she was nowhere in sight.

"Let's just go," I said.

Dad turned the car in a wide arc and drove us toward tarred, city roads. I sighed with relief when I heard the last crunch of gravel leave our tires. I wanted to believe I had escaped. When we got home I raced through the kitchen door calling out for my brand new puppy. "Cookie. Cookie. Where are you?"

Daddy stood at the kitchen door and hung his head. "Sister, Cookie isn't here," he said, his soft brown eyes pleading with me for understanding.

"Why not? Where is she?"

"I'm sorry honey. She got sick and we had to take her to the vet."

"When?"

"Yesterday."

"The whole litter got distemper," Mom interjected. "There was nothing we could do. She is going to die, Carol. I told the vet to wait until this afternoon in case you wanted to say goodbye."

"Yeah, I do," I said, working up my courage.

I was happy I got to hold Cookie in my arms one last time. Before I handed her back to the vet, she lost control of her bowels and runny green poop slid down my white cotton shirt.

Then I let go and cried.

12

When he first arrived at the hospital they made him take a bunch of tests before he met with Dr. Tyce, the head shrink from the Mayo Clinic, who took David Torgerson's history in their first visit.

> He asked me about the girl the one who turned blue. I told him about the others too: how the county had hauled me into court once or twice before for slapping stupid girls and there was them others I tried to drag from their yards. They wiggled away. I didn't touch their privates—nothing like that. They gave me probation and sent social workers to the house, which, of course, made my folks pretty mad. They took it out on me. I was the one who always got blamed for shit.
>
> Later, I told Tyce about that dumb-ass teacher. She's the reason I got put in Special Ed. Oh, it musta been sixth grade, sometime right round then. I'd got in trouble 'cuz I skipped a couple three months' worth of school—wasn't my fault. Everybody's always picking on me. So I threw a few books and cussed, stuff like that, nothin' big. I attended more regular the next couple of years, maybe only missed a day or so every other week. Still, they gave me D's. Said I didn't try. I

tried, hell yah, I tried. A guy like me just can't catch a break. Dr. Tyce told me I could get a diploma by taking more tests.

He likes me.

It didn't work out though—studying for tests b-o-r-i-n-g, plus it was too hard. Anybody could see that.

13

My seventh grade year was the loneliest one of my entire life. Austin split grades seven and eight. Kids from the Acres had to take the bus clear across town to attend Ellis, the newly-built junior high. Unlike Central Junior and Senior High, its staid three-story brick counterpart, Ellis, flat and modern, contained an interior quadrangle that stood silent except when the bell clanged. Then hundreds of boys and girls pushed and shoved their way across the transecting cement paths in a frantic attempt to get to their next class on time. Even when the weather was fair, no one sat on the cement benches that anchored each quadrant. The open-air courtyard flaunted a six-foot, black iron sculpture inset with brilliant red, yellow, blue, and green foot-wide glass orbs. After the grand unveiling, none of us gave the bejeweled monstrosity a second glance.

"Who is in my house?" Mom always called out from the basement whenever I walked through the kitchen door at the end of each school day.

"It's me," I said each time.

"Good. Grab a cookie and come down to tell me all about your day."

A mixture of detergent, bleach, hard water, and musk filled my nostrils as I stepped halfway down the wooden stairs to my usual spot. Mom loved doing the laundry and most especially the ironing. If she didn't have time to get it all done at once, she grabbed a green glass seven-up bottle filled with distilled water that was corked with an aluminum bottle stopper. She used it to sprinkle the left over clothes. She rolled up the whole rig-a-ma-roll, placed it in a zippered plastic bag, and then tossed the lot into the refrigerator.

Mom liked to hear about my day at school. She diligently kept all the names straight I chattered on about. Although she sometimes probed, I never shared any of the defining incidents of my junior high life with her. I hated lunch and recess most of all. The school cafeteria always swirled with moving bodies, but I could not find a welcoming face. I ate quickly before retreating to the haven of my next classroom doorway. A few other misfits gathered there, too. Janis wore her dull dark hair in a short bob and her complexion resembled cooked oatmeal. Claiming the classroom doorway as an inner sanctuary for us girls was Janis' daily ritual. She liked to put her muscular build to good use by ousting any puny seventh-grade boy foolish enough to dare an invasion. She jammed her solid butt into the doorway, spread her legs shoulder width apart, and placed one hand on each side of the plaster wall. Her legs held ground like two battle ships when she swung male intruders aside. Even when two or three of them came at her at once, she never lost control of the doorway. She couldn't have been fiercer if she had been defending newborn cubs. Even though I desperately wanted a best friend, or at least someone to eat lunch with, we were not destined to become buddies: she hated me for standing idly by as she fended off pimple-faced marauders.

"Carol, get in here and help me out!" she often spit across our divide. I studied the floor. Unlike me, Sybil Anderson occasionally lent Janis a hand. Because of her big-boned square build, boys often heckled she was built like a brick shithouse. I didn't care what they said. I thought she possessed raw beauty. Her straw-colored, straight, thick hair hung down to the middle of her back. She parted it on the side, so a hint of wave framed her oval face. Her olive eyes were surrounded with thick arched eyebrows and long curled dark lashes. Her mouth was set wide and generous. But the best part about Sybil was she needed a friend as much as I did. Soon we abandoned Janis. Even if Sybil sat down with other girls first, I knew the chair across from her was always saved for me. After grabbing a metal tray and sliding it down the runway of macaroni and cheese, sloppy joes and chocolate pudding, I picked up a milk carton, confident I could search the sea of faces for the safe harbor of Sybil's. I usually found her tucked in the back corner. We ate together, laughed together, and studied together. Knowing Sybil would be there whenever I entered the congested cafeteria made me breathe easier.

One day she invited me to come over to her house after school on Friday. For that special occasion, I wore a soft blue angora sweater, a straight black skirt that fell just below my knees, and black leather flats. I felt terribly happy as we walked the dozen or so blocks to her house—a squat, nondescript white stucco bungalow. The front door led directly into the living room packed full with comfy overstuffed chairs and a matching couch. The house's most charming feature was its arched opening flanked by bookcases that separated the living room from the dining room. No one seemed to be home when we arrived. Sybil fetched cookies and milk from the kitchen and we settled in at the dining room table. Before long a car drove up the side of the house. Two car doors slammed and the kitchen door swung open as Sybil's mother bustled into the kitchen with a young boy following closely on her heels. Her arms were laden with three brown grocery bags. Standing nearly six feet tall, she reminded me of a bell tower. Her massive body was almost as wide as it is tall. I waited to be introduced.

"Mom, this is Carol."

"Hello, Mrs. Anderson," I said, polite as possible.

"Nice to meet you. What is your last name, dear?" she asked.

"Haack."

"Huh. Is your mom Lois?" "Uh huh," I said smiling. "Do you know her?"

Just then Doug, Sybil's 15-year-old brother, tromped down the stairs. His bare feet slapped on the linoleum as he rounded the corner. He stopped short staring at me. Leaning into the doorjamb, his look lingered. Starting with my face, he let his eyes travel down my body then back up before stopping at my developing chest. I peeked at his tousled hair, bare chest, and flannel pajama bottoms.

His lips formed a smirk. "Who's this?" he asked of no one in particular.

I blushed. Embarrassment skated up my spine, reaching all the way to my hairline.

Before I could escape into the kitchen, I noticed Mrs. Anderson gaze intently in my direction.

"Douglas, get your butt back upstairs and get dressed," she commanded. "Then come down here and help me unload the groceries."

Sybil and I sat next to each other in the living room watching TV until we were called to supper. No one talked much at their table other than to say pass the peas please. After helping with the dishes, I called my mom to drive over to pick me up. The following Monday I eagerly looked for Sybil in the school cafeteria. I smiled as I approached our usual table.

"Don't sit down."

"What?"

"You can't sit with me," Sybil said, avoiding my eyes. "My mother says I should never talk to you again."

"What?" I said again, staring at her in disbelief.

"She says you are *that* girl and I need to stay away from you. We can't be friends anymore. That's all."

"Oh, Okay," I stammered before walking across the noisy cafeteria to throw my lunch away. We never looked in each other's direction again.

14

Miss Nobel, my eighth grade English teacher, and Miss Winslow, my home economics teacher, were roommates. I loved English and hated home economics, which was mandatory for all eighth grade girls. Unlike most of my classmates, I had no intention of taking home economics as an elective in the ninth grade. I had a crush on Miss Nobel. I considered her beautiful, although by most any standard she clearly was not. At five-feet-five she comfortably tipped the scales at well over two hundred fifty pounds. She always wore wide, flowing black A-line skirts, and her black patent high heels clicked as she walked up and down the rows of our class. Her ebony hair, cut so short it fit her skull like a cap, glistened. Miss Winslow's defining features included slightly wild strawberry permed hair, tortoise shell glasses dangling from a chain around her neck, and a gap between her squared-off top front teeth.

In Miss Nobel's class, we read and discussed stories, studied grammar, vocabulary, and compiled book reports. During the week of Halloween, Miss Nobel decided we should hone our public speaking skills. On the day of our first speech, she lectured about the importance of establishing eye contact with our audience, cautioned us to wait until we had command of the podium before opening our mouths, and urged us to talk slow and loud so we could be heard from the last row where she would be sitting. After clickity-clacking to the back of the class to take a seat, she opened her black grade book and announced the impromptu subject: "Students, I want you to describe your scariest experience. I will give you five minutes to prepare."

The blood drained from my face, making me look as if I had actually seen a ghost. I felt faint. One-by-one, my classmates raised their hands to volunteer. Spooky basements, eerie campouts, scary walks beside cemeteries, anxious performances, and getting lost or left behind on family outings, represented the typical junior high experiences shared on that first day. Brad Deters told about going into his basement to fetch some laundry for his mother. He panicked over hearing a bang and a whooshing sound. When he turned he saw flames like the gates of hell licking out of the holes in a metal gate from the cast iron furnace. Either a ghost or the devil was after him. He said he climbed the stairs two at a time and tripped over his own feet, which he demonstrated on the way back to his seat. The class laughed. He was such a clown. Arlo Saunders rose to outdo Brad's story. He described how, on a trip out West with his family, he became frightened listening to the rustle and scamper of feet in the woods outside the perimeter of their campsite. His father told him it was a snipe and nothing to be afraid of. He offered to take any of us girls on a snipe hunt if we wanted to go. Some of the boys smirked and snickered. I didn't know why. Renee Heimsness talked about how having to make this speech scared her to death. Miss Nobel acknowledged this was true for almost everyone. She said research showed Americans feared public speaking ahead of dying.

Slim comfort.

The bell rang signaling the end of class and we all rushed from the room while Miss Nobel yelled out, "Students, we will finish up tomorrow."

On the bus ride home that afternoon, Susie Wright slid into the seat beside me and said, "Lucky you. You have the perfect story to tell in English class tomorrow."

"You think so?"

"Yeah, it'll be great. I have always wanted to know one thing though."

"What's that?"

"Well," Susie said, she often punctuated her sentences with 'well.' "Why didn't you scream? Our house was only a half block around the bend. We might a heard yah, you know."

Mute, I gazed out the bus window. Now, along with being *that* girl, I was the girl who could have saved herself if she had just screamed.

Walking through the classroom door the next day, I hoped and prayed Miss Nobel had forgotten yesterday's assignment. But after taking roll, she clip-clopped to the empty seat in the back, opened her black grade book, and waited for one of us to volunteer. One-by-one the rest of the class stood up and delivered. I spoke last. I rubbed my sweaty palms down the sides of my skirt as I walked those four solitary steps to the front of the room. My mouth and throat grew dry. I hesitated. Susie, who always sat in the front row so she could be closest to the teacher, beamed at me. Encouraged, I began to share my story.

"When I was ten, I went on a summer picnic. My twin brother went too, but he stopped to play touch football so I was on my own." I paused, cast my eyes to the floor, and licked my lips. "When I got to the woods, this guy came out and asked me for directions to Sunnyside Avenue. I was real polite when I told him he was lost. 'We only have rural route one, rural route two, no street names,' I explained. After I walked away, he came up behind me and put his hands around my throat. He lifted me off the ground saying, 'Don't scream,' and then he squeezed his hands real tight around my neck." I swallowed hard. "He strangled me until I passed out. When I woke up, blood covered my tummy and I, I was rolled in barbed wire hanging off the hill above Turtle Creek and …"

The tension rose in the room like a hot air balloon. Judging by my classmate's faces and stiff posture, I could see I had truly scared them. I scuffed my toe on the linoleum. Miss Nobel cleared her throat. While studying her grade book, she mumbled I had earned my grade and told me to take my seat. Somehow this incident did not daunt my enthusiasm for English class or Miss Nobel. Having a positive experience in Home Ec class didn't make me any fonder of Miss Winslow either.

A fitting laboratory for divining the domestic arts of cooking and sewing, our adjoining home economics classrooms covered one whole side of the hall. There was a full kitchen with seven round tables for dining, a lecture-style classroom with four rows of seven desks, and a mock living room that faced twenty-eight sewing stations. Large windows graced each room with natural light. After Miss Winslow demonstrated a simple recipe, each small group replicated it. Waiting for the food to cook, we set our respective tables' properly—knife and spoon to the right, salad and dinner forks on the left, soup spoon laid horizontal with the top of the plate. At the end of the first quarter of culinary instruction, each one of us was required to prepare a meal at home for our respective families. To fulfill this dreaded homework assignment, I decided to make cream of potato soup and a jellyroll for supper. Ever dutiful, I carried home the evaluation sheet that accompanied the assignment, which included categories to be graded such as appearance, texture, and taste. Threatening to go on a hunger strike, Curt complained about having to eat anything I prepared. My confidence tumbled further. After Dad gave him a stern look, he grudgingly sat down at the kitchen table. Dad slurped my soup willingly, even though, as a meat and potatoes man, soup did not rank high on his list.

Although Mom excelled in the art of cooking, her jellyrolls always crumbled and split apart. That night, mine was texture perfect. Mom liked my jellyroll so much she asked me for the recipe—high praise. I felt proud there was a recipe only I could master.

"Here is my critique of your efforts," Mom said the next morning as she handed me a sealed envelope. I obediently placed it in the basket on the teacher's desk as Miss Winslow walked down the aisle at the beginning of class. While we were occupied with taking a multiple choice exam, Miss Winslow sat at her desk reading all of the parent evaluations. Near the end of the hour, she announced that she wanted to read one special evaluation out loud. Opening a lined piece of paper, she recited, 'Ode to a Jelly Roll.' This rhyming limerick described the baking process with lines such as, 'flour on her nose' and the final lines partnered 'I couldn't have more pride' with 'when she makes jellyroll as a bride.' My classmates clapped as Miss Winslow walked to my desk to return it to me. Mom's heart-felt tribute to my culinary efforts made me glow.

Learning to sew took up half of the Home Economics curriculum. For my first sewing project, I used brown embroidery thread to slip-stitch a pattern onto the end of a yellow kitchen towel. Next I tackled a poncho, which required only one seam and no zipper. I chose a Scotch wool plaid and lined it with navy cotton. I looked forward to wearing it to fall 'Packer' football games. We all advanced to a more involved sewing project in the spring. Each of us was required to make a two-piece Easter outfit to model at our spring fashion show, a cumulative event held to showcase our domestic skills where we would be serving scones and tea to all of our moms. I selected lilac linen material out of the bin in the back of the sewing lab. Although I handled the first two sewing projects fairly well, when I tried to sew the zipper into the skirt, the tension in the bobbin grew taut causing the needle to whirr to a halt. I raised my hand to get Miss Winslow's attention.

"What's the matter, Carol?" she asked after walking across the room to stand by my side. "The needle is stuck."

A quick examination revealed the problem. "You've sewn the zipper clear through to the front of your skirt. Why didn't you stop when you felt the bobbin tighten?" she said in exasperation.

I shrugged.

After motioning me to give up my seat, she sat and raised her glasses up from the chain that held them around her neck in order to examine my hapless garment. She released the lever, manually reversed the needle from the fabric, and then withdrew her sharp scissors from a pocket in her smock. After a couple of quick snips, the garment was freed.

"Go over in the corner and rip out all of these stitches while I rethread your bobbin," Miss Winslow directed, pulling another tool from her pocket and handing it over to me. I spent the rest of the week painstakingly removing hundreds of tiny, tight stitches that traversed through the zipper clear through to the front of my A-line skirt. Occasionally, Miss Winslow peered over my shoulder to gauge my progress. When I finally finished removing the zipper, she grabbed my skirt and properly inserted the zipper in less than a minute. All I needed to do now was sew on the hook and eye closure at the waistband. However, now my skirt looked like dotted Swiss instead of smooth linen. Numerous needle-sized holes spewed diagonally across the front of the skirt, and then gathered force, ending in a Milky-way swirl at the most indelicate position possible. This would never do. I had shown my true ineptness as a future homemaker and the fashion show was scheduled for the next day. My debacle gave Miss Winslow the opportunity to prove she was as dedicated as Miss Jean Brodie when it came to preparing her charges for the vicissitudes of domestic bliss.

"Too bad you picked linen," she grumbled. "It is not very forgiving," She stood and clapped her hands twice. "Girls, gather round while I show you how to restore damaged material," she said, taking my crumpled, pitiful skirt to the ironing board where she placed dampened cheesecloth over the pin holes and pressed down hard with the iron. The heat and the steam helped to tighten some of the holes in the blemished cloth, but the result only pointed out what I already knew—once damaged, the fabric of our lives is forever altered.

15

Just before Christmas break of my eighth grade year, I sat by myself gazing out the frosty bus window. After dropping Susie Wright off, the bus rambled around the bend. As we approached Martha Cleveland's' house, I noticed someone standing at the end of the next driveway wearing a knit cap and a tan and black checkered wool jacket, zipped tight. His hands were tucked away in his pants pockets. Soft snow flakes settled on his head and shoulders.

The brakes emitted a familiar groan as the driver pushed down on the pedal. Grinding to a stop, the bus lurched forward then back. Martha grabbed the seat back in front of mine to steady herself. I followed her eyes as they darted to the lone figure approaching their adjoining mailboxes. The color washed from her face. After regaining her balance, she clutched her school books tight to her chest. I felt tension slice through her body as she moved toward the bus's rear exit.

Looking over his shoulder, the bus driver's right arm hung in mid-motion. With a quick adjustment, he moved his hand away from grabbing the lever that opened the front door and instead pressed on the red button in order to operate the rear exit. I watched Martha gallop through the blank snow. She reached her front door before the bus back exit door clanged shut. Cold air registered on the back of my neck at the same time the bundled figure reached my window. Lifting an ungloved hand to touch my windowpane, he looked directly into my eyes and smiled.

I shivered. Even though it had been two-and-a-half years since I last saw him walking down Austin's court house corridor, I knew those glasses—his face. I was a little girl then, I thought to myself, how could he recognize me now?

The bus sputtered and jerked as the driver engaged the engine. My stomach plunged in sync. I steadied myself by holding onto the round steel bar topping the seat back in front of mine. My fingers clamped down as my chest grew tight. I held my breath. Worried he might try to board the bus at the next stop, I swiveled in my seat to take in the clear view out of the big rear window. Torgerson's brown shoes stood still in the crusted snow as he lifted his right hand to wave goodbye. I continued my frozen vigil for more than a dozen blocks before my breathing returned to normal. When the bus chugged to a stop at my house, I rushed inside.

"Who's in my house?" Mom called out in our usual routine.

I clambered down the basement steps without stopping to remove my coat.

"Mom, David's back," I said. "He came right up to the bus and smiled at me through the window."

"It couldn't be him, Carol," Mom said, looking up from her ironing. "We have a court order that says we would be notified if he is ever released."

"It was him, Mom. I saw him," I said my voice raising an octave. "He walked right up to my window! He knows me."

"Okay, Okay. Calm down," she said while pulling the plug on the iron. "I'll make a call and see what's going on."

After we reached the top of the basement stairs she motioned for me to sit down at the kitchen table. I heard my parent's bureau drawer scrape open and close from the back of the house.

"Here it is," she said, placing a manila file and her reading glasses on our black Formica table before slipping a cigarette out of her ready pack of Salem Menthols, which she lit from the gas burner on the stove. "Just let me get a cup of coffee here and then I'll be ready."

I remained quiet and still except for my twitching fingers. Placing one over the other, I folded my hands into my lap as Mom shuffled through the file. She removed a page and scanned it for a moment.

"Here, read me the number," she instructed, tapping the top of the letterhead as she stood to grab the receiver off our wall phone. Taking a deep breath I recited, "4-3-7-55-00."

"This is Mrs. Haack. Can I speak to Mr. Kelley?" Mom said into the phone and smiled at me as she waited.

"Yes, hello Mr. Kelley. This is Mrs. Haack. My daughter Carol tells me that David Torgerson is home. Is that true?"

Disdain spread across her face.

"Uh, huh. How long?" she asked pursing her lips. "Well, what about my daughter? Why weren't we notified? I thought we had a court order if he was released," she said with some heat to her voice. She hung up the phone, turned to face me and said in her no nonsense voice, "He's home for two weeks so you won't be going anywhere alone during Christmas break."

Later that night I overheard her tell Dad, "He said, 'If she were my daughter, I'd keep her under lock and key.' A fine kettle of fish, we are supposed to keep her locked up!"

Decades later, Curt told me he had bumped into Wayne Torgerson, David's brother, in the school locker room the day after the bus incident. Curt had just left the shower and popped open the military beige locker where his clothes were stashed when he heard the next class of boys enter. Head down, a boy muttered, "S'cuse me," as he scooted past the white-toweled butt standing next to my twin brother.

"Sure thing," Curt replied turning sideways to let him pass, which was when their eyes locked. Startled, the two boys sized each other up. No contest. Curt, muscled from lifting weights for wrestling, could bench press three of Wayne.

Curt's blue eyes flashed dark as ink as his jaw set. "I hear your brother's home."

"Yeah, he's home for holidays," Wade nodded, and then looked away.

"Well, you tell **him** if he comes near my sister I'm gonna beat the shit outta 'im!" Curt said, leaning forward to stab a finger into Wade's puny chest. "You got that?"

"Yup. You know," Wade said, bringing his pained eyes up to meet Curt's dancing angry ones, "if you think being her brother is hard, you should try being his."

> Dumb ass Christmas holiday. It don't matter. God-damn-it-to-hell.

"Harold, they're releasing David," Esther Torgerson said.

"Whadda ya mean?"

"They want us to come get him next week," Esther said handing her husband a letter from Rochester State Mental Hospital. "He's served his time."

"I don't want him. We made him a ward of the state."

Harold grimaced as he scanned the letter. "Look at this. Says he choked a girl, a patient, up there a couple of months ago. What the hell…"

The Torgerson family was not alone in their dismay over their eldest son's return home. Their next door neighbor, Gerald Cleaveland, who owned the local hardware store, remembered all too well having to keep a vigilant eye on his only child, Martha. How that Torgerson boy dragged her out of their front yard when she was only five and he was ten. Scared them almost half to death. Good thing Martha had a good set of lungs on her, Cleaveland considered, or the wife would never have been alerted. Even though Martha was a teenager now and a promising athlete, Gerald and his wife were worried sick.

"This morning Harold told me David's back for good. Harold can't believe it either," Gerald said to his wife over Sunday morning coffee. "I'm going to talk this over with Judge Plunket next time we play golf. People shouldn't have to live like this."

"Yes, you must do something, dear. I love this house but we can't live next to them, not after what that boy did to the poor Haack girl. He's only been gone for three years for heaven's sake. Something's got to be done or we're putting this house on the market!"

Judge Plunket thought something should be done about Torgerson's release too. As soon as his golf chum, Gerald Cleaveland, told him Torgerson had returned he marched right off the green to call Sven Olson, the county sheriff.

"What the hell's going on, Sven?" the judge shrieked. "Cleaveland tells me David Torgerson's been let go! Did you know about this?"

"No, sir."

"I sent that boy away for good. Made sure his commitment papers said, 'a danger to the public,' and those fools over there in Rochester just up and let him go. This is not gonna happen, not on my watch!" Judge Plunket sputtered. "Go pick that Torgerson boy up. Take him back today. Yah, hear? I'll call over to Rochester and tell 'em you're on the way."

"Yes sir, I'm on it, your Honor."

> The sheriff showed up a couple of weeks after I got home. Told my folks how it was all this big fat-ass mistake. Only gave me a half-hour to pack stuff, say good-bye. The drive back took less than an hour. In-take was the same as before—something like that's bound to crank up the pressure cooker on a guy. After I got back, Dr. Tyce told me I'm gonna get out a here after my next birthday. You'll be grown up then. Dr. Tyce don't lie neither.

A week after he was returned to the hospital from his short-lived, unlawful release, Torgerson throttled a second female patient for refusing his flirtatious advances. This outburst earned him another stint in the locked ward.

> She smiled at me when I passed her in the hallway. A pretty girl, nice boobs. I walked right up and kissed her. The bitch—she pushed me away. Yelled. Called me a dirty name. If she hadn't done that everything been just fine—just a reflex, putting my hands up to her neck like that. Her fault really. She screamed bloody murder so them orderlies, they came running.

16

Being a bus kid turned a 15-minute trip into an hour's ordeal. The relentless rhythm of the bus created a cruel monotony. I disliked the smell of diesel fuel, the guttural chug of the engine, and the whine of the hydraulic brakes that accompanied each stop and start. In order to open and close the front door, the driver had to reach way over to pull or push the iron lever. With each execution, the door gasped. Even without the boisterous bickering of its occupants, the bus's continual lurching made it impossible to sleep or read. Sometimes Susie or some other girl sat with me but one spring day, while I was daydreaming with my forehead resting on the dusty window pane, I saw two hands grab the bar on the back of the seat in front of me, and then I felt the black vinyl bench give way.

A boy plopped himself down right beside me. Surprised, I gave a quick glance around and noticed two vacant benches along with a number of open spots next to other boys. Why would he sit here, I wondered? His eyes faced forward while the bus lumbered along. Although neither of us said a word, an electric tension bounced along with us. My stomach felt queasy. When the bus slowed curbside, everyone jostled for position. Colors blurred as kids ran every which way off to class. I forgot all about it during the bustle of the day. Then, on the ride home, he plopped his butt right down beside me again. As the bus filled up, one boy giggled and punched him in the ribs when he walked past our seat. A couple of girls, who were sitting near the front of the bus, twirled their heads around and stared in my direction.

"My name is Al," he said, right before the bus stopped to let him off at his house. "Save me a seat in the morning, Okay?"

I didn't think I really needed to save him a seat no one else wanted anyway, but I nodded and then watched him walk up the aisle to the exit. I peered out the window as the bus took off. Before walking up his drive, he stopped, turned, and then he waved at me through the haze of the exhaust.

When he walked down the aisle the next morning, I noticed he wore his straight jet-black hair parted on the side. He slid into the seat next to me as if it was the most natural thing in the world to do.

"Thanks for saving me a seat," he said, flashing a grateful smile.

I stole a sideways look—his eyes were the color of deep roasted coffee, just like Dad's.

"What's your name?" he asked me.
"Carol."
"What grade are you in?"
"Ninth."
"Me too. What's your first hour class?"
"Civics."
"With Steffan's?"
"Yah."
"I have him fifth period."

Having exhausted his repertoire of small talk, we rode the rest of the way in silence. After the bus arrived, he moved into the aisle before saying, "I'll sit with you on the way home."

Oh, my gosh, I think he likes me. He really must like me. In all the time that I wanted a best friend, I never once thought it might be a boy. For the first time in my life, I am eager to take the bus. That afternoon, I bounced up the three steps and skipped down the aisle to our seat. Sitting on the outside of the bench, he stood to let me in. Crawling past him into the window seat, our hands grazed.

"Did Steffan assign a test to your class too?" he asked.

"Uh-huh."

"Get off the bus with me at my house. We can study together. I will walk you home after."

"Okay. But I gotta tell my brother so he can tell my mom."

The bus chugged to a stop and four of us got off. A couple of girls, whose names I did not know, jumped free along with Al and me and walked up the road about five feet. Bright sunshine danced around my head as the bus rumbled down the road.

"Here. Let me take your books," Al said. "My house is the white one over there."

As I handed over my books one of the girls called out, "Al, can we talk to you in private?"

"Sure," he said, before turning back to me. "Wait right here. This won't take long."

And it didn't. Within two minutes it was all over. Al's smiling face flushed red with anger as he thrust my books back into my arms.

"Cheryl says you are *that* girl. Why didn't you tell me you were *that* girl!"

"What girl?" I croaked.

"The one who teased her boyfriend in the woods then sent him to jail," he spat. "I don't want to have anything to do with you!"

Dazed and speechless, I watched him march off to join Cheryl and the other girl, who waited to watch it all unfold. I headed for home fast. I didn't want Curt to get their first. When I opened the kitchen door, Mom called out her customary, "Who's in my house?"

"It's me," I said, my voice steady.

"Get a cookie from the counter and some milk and come down and tell me all about your day."

"There's not much to tell," I muttered sitting on the bare stair step. "We have a test in civics tomorrow. That's all."

"Go. Bring your book down then, too. You can study while I iron."

The next morning I kept my head down, burying my nose in my civics textbook so I could pretend I didn't notice Al and Cheryl sitting together on the bus. I aced my civics test with the highest score in my class: 99 out of 100.

17

When she was seventeen, Lana Iverson was arrested as a transient. Subsequently, Olmsted County Welfare Department sent her to Rochester State Mental Hospital for a diagnostic work-up. Her evaluation took six-weeks—long enough for her to meet David Torgerson. At first, Torgerson wasn't sure Iverson was his type because she had slim hips and a flat chest.

Dr. Joyce Bickford administered the Shipley-Hartford Assessment (an instrument which measures intellectual and conceptual knowledge) to Lana Iverson. Her overall IQ came in at 64. David Torgerson's IQ, assessed by the Wechsler Adult Intelligence Scale when he was first admitted to the mental hospital, measured 73. Dr. Bickford also diagnosed Lana as having a situational personality disorder, adjustment reaction to adolescence. Psychiatric double-talk for rebellious teenager.

In his first years at Rochester State Mental Hospital, David Torgerson worked as an attendant at the hospital laundry. Later, he worked across town at Rochester's Ability Building Center, a sheltered workshop for the mentally challenged. In December of 1965, Torgerson's job there was disrupted when he kissed a worker against her will. In spite of this, Torgerson would work at ABC on-and-off for the next three years. This sheltered work shop setting would end up being the most stable vocational experience of his life.

Lana Iverson's short, tangled hair resembled the tasseled end of an ear of corn. Dishwater blonde, its dark roots were a clear sign of a bad home dye job. Even though the female and male residents of Rochester's Mental Hospital ate in separate dining hall sections, Lana sidled up to Torgerson's table at dinner one night.

"Hi," she said, in a saucy voice. "What's your name?"

He looked up, surprised. Before he could open his mouth, she giggled and said, "Where you been all my life, good lookin'?"

He looked around to see if she was trying to make a fool out of him—show off for her friends or something. It had happened to him plenty of times before. But that would become the thing he came to like about her the best—she didn't play games behind his back. If she was mad, he knew it. Most times, she was happy, though. She laughed a lot.

"David," he said. "My name's David, David Torgerson. How 'bout you?"

"Lana, I ain't seen you round here much in the day. How come?"

"I go to work. I work off campus," he bragged, looking her up and down. "You here long?"

"Bickford's given me bunch a tests. You know her? She's the one looks like she been eating sour pickles." Lana pulled her cheeks in, puckered up her lips, and then they both laughed out loud.

"Iverson!" the matron yelled across the dining hall. "Get over here."

"Oops, caught me," she said, flashing a goofy grin.

He saw that her top teeth were slightly crossed. He had a quarter-inch gap between his own. When she started to walk away, he stood, grabbed her arm. She turned, looked up at him with eyes as big as a blue plate special.

"I like you," he said. "You wanna kiss, make out sometime?"

She laughed, put her arms around his waist, bumped her hip against his, and he was a goner.

During group therapy sessions Dr. Bickford didn't mince her words. "You're a trouble-maker, Iverson. A flirt. Stubborn and immature," she said, her face red as a ripe tomato. "If you don't quit sneaking around with that Torgerson, you're going to end up in trouble—pregnant. He's seven years older than you. The rules are meant to protect you. Start following them!"

Lana crossed her eyes and stuck out her tongue as soon as Dr. Bickford turned her back and the rest of the girls tittered. Two weeks later Dr. Bickford had her mal-adjusted, adolescent ass hauled off to the Lino Lakes Home for Girls, located a little north of the twin cities and a straight drive up 35W.

"Tell me how this week has been working out for you?" Torgerson's psychiatrist, Dr. Tyce, asked. This was how he began every therapy session with every patient.

"I met a girl."

"We've talked about this before, David," Dr. Tyce said, not looking up from his note pad. "You need to leave girls alone."

"Yup. Her name's Lana, Lana Iverson. I make her laugh."

"David, pay attention," Tyce said, giving Torgerson a thin smile. "The paper work from Mower County we talked about should be here soon. Remember? Then you'll have more freedom. That's our goal. You want that don't you?"

"Yes," David replied meekly. He never fought with Dr. Tyce—looked up to him actually. Men did not make Torgerson angry the way women did. It don't matter much, Torgerson thought, Lana's leaving soon anyway,

"During your provisional release you'll still live at the hospital—but in 'A' ward. You'll need to check in there by ten in the evening for the first year," Dr. Tyce said, bringing David back into the present. "You can continue to work at ABC while you look for work in the community. This is a big opportunity for you, David, you do need to show us that you can control the symptoms that brought you here. Understand? Of course, we will still meet like this, every other week, to monitor your progress."

"Yup," Torgerson responded trying to look as if he had been listening all along.

> Next time I see Lana I gotta get her number
> so I can call her up when I get outta here.
> She's my girl.

Throughout the eighteen months of his provisional release, Torgerson dutifully attended each of his alternating Friday therapy sessions with Dr. Tyce. However, they never discussed the rage building up inside of him. In the late spring of 1968, on a directive from Dr. Tyce, Rochester State Mental Hospital petitioned Mower County to have the magic words, 'a danger to the public,' removed from Torgerson's court commitment papers. Torgerson's new Wechsler assessment score of 83 was included in the request, along with a peculiar statement from the certified tester who reported he felt Torgerson's actual ability was closer to 100.

David Torgerson stopped seeing Dr. Tyce and moved fully back into the community. With few real skills he had trouble finding and keeping work. He stocked shelves at Lawry's Wholesale Produce Market, carried luggage at the Kahler Hotel, and stood on the line at Libby's Corn. By then, David Torgerson and Lana Iverson had become a hot item.

18

I picked up extra classes in my sophomore and junior years, which allowed me to work full time during my senior year of high school. I attended school from eight until noon and then walked to Woolworth's on Main Street to punch the time clock. Most days my shift lasted until eight p.m. but I got Wednesday and Friday nights off and didn't have to work at all on Sunday. Throughout the time my family lived in the Acres, Mom sporadically announced, "Tonight's family night. If you have plans, cancel them."

We all knew better than to protest.

"You need good grades to get into college. We expect you to do well in school," Mom said each time before bringing out the cards, Monopoly, or Sorry for our family activity.

Teddy did. Named a National Merit Scholar, he earned a full ride to Macalester College in Saint Paul. Mom and Dad were proud.

"So what's going on in school this week," Mom said like she always did at the start of each family night. Curt talked about phys-ed and shop and for a while I chatted about my English, German, and Forensic classes. "I have been accepted to all of the colleges I applied to," I finally said placing five envelopes on the table. "Concordia offered a thousand dollar scholarship but it's so far away. Macalester too, but I don't want to follow Teddy Bob anymore and…"

"You're not going to college," Mom interrupted.

"Huh? You always talked about working hard to get good grades to go to college. I…"

"That was for the boys, you're a girl."

My heart beat fast. I slipped a letter out from its envelope and read out loud from it, 'Your SAT score puts you in the ninety-second percentile across this nation. You should attend college.'

"I wa-a-nt to go on to school," I stuttered. "I can attend a state school. It's cheaper and…"

Mom shook her head no.

"What am I supposed to do after I graduate?" I asked her.

"Take secretarial training and get a job," she said. "That's what I always wanted."

"I can't!" I whined. "Typing… that's my only 'D.' I'm no good at it!" I sobbed. My tears joined with the snot dripping out of my nose.

After a tense silence Dad cleared his throat. "Let the girl go."

"Okay, maybe she'll get a better husband," Mom said, pursing her lips, "but you have to live at home. Go to the junior college and pay your own way."

For my freshman year I waitressed at the local truck stop; night shift, 10:00 p.m. to 8:00 a.m., and then took back-to-back classes from 9:00 to 1:00. In 1967, my sophomore year, I transferred colleges and lived on campus, which was when David Torgerson started to spend his days off campus—voluntarily returning to Rochester State Mental Hospital at night during his provisional release.

A dozen years later, when she lay dying, Mom told me, "You weren't ready. I wasn't ready. Seventeen was too young to leave home. Academically, sure, they even wanted to jump you a grade in elementary school. I said 'no,' you were a twin. That first year, after you went away to college, I'd see your empty closet and just sink. I'd sit on your bed and cry. After a while I stopped going into your room. It was easier.

You have been the best daughter anyone could ever want. Well, except for the prom, I was mad at you for not going. I wanted to buy you the prettiest dress, take pictures. Seems silly—so unimportant now. I was always worried you were too sensitive to make it in the world, you know. But I have come to see you are the emotionally strongest of all my children."

I sat silent, my sorrow too big for words.

Part Two

We don't see things as they are; we see them as we are.

~Anais Nin

19

Charlotte Jarrett July 13, 1968

> All I took was a white button from her shirt.

Setting her half-smoked menthol cigarette on the bathroom sink, Charlotte tipped the bottle of Cover Girl, sheer classic ivory, into her palm before dabbing a splotch on her forehead, cheeks, and chin. Her boss called her doll face—a nod to her porcelain complexion. Saturday evening shifts promised to be better than staying home with Milo. Yesterday, like he did on most Friday nights, he'd come home late, three-sheets-to-the-wind. Charlotte had left his place set at the table. When Milo showed his face, Bobby and Carly, bathed and in their pajama's, quietly slipped away from the yellow Formica table and scurried into their bedroom to play.

"What's for dinner?" he had growled.

"The kids had Mac-n-Cheese and Sloppy Joes," Charlotte said, holding her breath. "There's some of that left."

"How 'bout a steak? Fry me up one."

"No steak," Charlotte replied, biting her lower lip. She turned her back to him and began fussing with the dishes.

Although the windows were open, the gingham curtains hung perfectly still. Tension inched up Charlotte's slight frame like a caterpillar on tree bark.

"Charlotte, Goddamn-it-to-hell, I'm talking to you here," Milo slurred. "Quit swashing them damn dishes and answer me!"

Charlotte pursed her lips and mopped her sweaty brow with the back of her hand. It wouldn't matter what she said now. She could tell he was lookin' for a fight.

"I'm a man, not some whiney snot-nosed kid," he bellowed. "You just answer me that one why doncha?" Milo said, nostrils flaring.

Remaining mute, Charlotte blew a wisp of hair off her forehead. Milo grabbed the empty plate resting at his elbow and sailed it across the kitchen. Charlotte swirled to face him, a reflex action. Soapy dish in hand, she lifted her chin and opened her fingers letting the bowl drop to the floor. Not wanting to be outdone, Milo pulled the full dish drain onto the floor and then swayed over to the refrigerator. Reaching up he snatched the carnival plate off the top. The cobbled plate's orange-gold iridescence flashed under the florescent light as he held it high above his head.

"Don't! That's my plate!" Bobby howled from the doorframe. "I won that for Mom at the fair." Tears poured down his cherry cheeks as he implored, "Ple-e-a-s-e, Daddy, don't break it."

Milo's chest heaved in the gaping silence. He fell against the counter and cast his bleary eyes, brimmed with shame, to the floor. He placed the plate on the counter then stumbled off to bed without another word. Charlotte welcomed Bobby with an open arm as she returned the treasured plate to its secure spot on top of the Frigidaire.

"How 'bout we jump into bed," Charlotte soothed stooping to whisper in her son's ear. "And I'll read you and Carly a bed time story. Okay?"

Sighing, Charlotte shook off last night's memory as she blinked her lashes triple-time. She didn't want to smear her mascara. She straightened the collar on her blouse then smoothed her skirt at the hip. No sense in being late for work, she reasoned. They needed the extra income and Michael's was the best waitress job in town.

When Charlotte drove her car into the Kahler parking garage she noticed a slight man wandering about on the first floor. For a moment their eyes locked. His looked almost black. She'd seen dark, angry eyes like that before when Milo was about to explode. Feeling uneasy, Charlotte drove all the way to the fifth floor to park. As soon as she stepped out of her car, she adjusted her straight black skirt and ran her fingers through her honey colored hair before entering the ramp's stairway. Even though she was the mother of two, Charlotte had managed to keep her figure trim. She was proud of that. Being pretty and petite helped in the tip department too. Often, a customer pressed a five buck tip into her hand. Lord knows a waitress could not survive on the wages paid out in a restaurant. Starting down the steps to the hotel lobby, Charlotte saw the guy she'd spied from the first floor climbing up the stairs. She paused, and then shrugged her shoulders. She couldn't be late.

He brushed past her. He didn't say a word: came up behind her and pushed his hands tight around her neck. Charlotte struggled, managed to scream.

Shut up bitch.

He took her down; squeezed harder like she was a kernel of stinking corn. David Torgerson felt a soft pop and then something in her throat gave way before he cracked her head against the cement stairwell. Three times: thwack, thwack, thunk. It was easy like smashing a pumpkin.

Purple. Dead.

He straddled her hips, leaned forward and unbuttoned the top three buttons of her starched white shirt.

Cindy Evers, a student nurse, drew near the elevator area. She heard the ding of the car as it approached from the floor below. Glancing to her left, she saw a man walk to the door that led outside. A moment later, a woman appeared staggering toward the elevator.

"I've been strangled," the woman croaked, her voice almost inaudible. "Help me."

Cindy steadied her as best she could until the elevator car binged and its door opened. After they shuffled inside, Cindy picked up the parking garage phone and punched zero.

"Call the police," Cindy said to the switchboard operator. "A woman's been attacked on the top floor of the garage. I'm bringing her down now."

Officers Olson and Caron responded to the 911 call from the Kahler. They found a dazed woman resting on the couch in the lobby. They placed her between them and escorted her to their squad car. Charlotte Jarrett gripped the officers' sturdy concerned arms. Officer Caron settled next to her in the back seat. She rested her head on his broad shoulder as the car, sirens blaring, delivered her to Methodist Hospital. Detective Bruesk was waiting for them in the emergency room when they arrived. It was his case.

"Can you answer a couple questions, ma'am?" Detective Bruesk asked notebook in hand. After supplying the basics (name, age, address), Charlotte gave a detailed description of her attacker: between the ages of 25 and 30; around 5'10" with a medium build; thick, dark, wavy hair; glasses with dark rims; an unshaven chin.

Charlotte shuddered. "He wore a red, white, blue, and yellow plaid sport shirt and dark wash-and-wear trousers."

"Ever see this guy before?" Bruesk asked. "Think you could identify 'em?

"I know I can," Charlotte said with confidence. "Seeing him once was enough. I'll never forget his face."

"Alright then," Bruesk smiled. "Here's my card. You call and come on down to the station house when you're ready. I'll pull some mug shots."

Back at the station house Officer Daly was taking a statement from Cindy Evers, who confirmed Charlotte's description of the attacker's height, body build, hair, and that the man had been wearing glasses. The only difference between the two accounts was age: Cindy took him to be younger, around nineteen or twenty.

After flipping through dozens of pages of unflattering photos, Charlotte Jarrett paused and pointed, "This isn't the guy... but he kinda looks like him except for the goatee."

Bruesk studied the photo. Kinda looks like Don Roch, he thought. Yup, he's a bad-ass petty thief and all around thug. He coulda done it.

"Wait right here," Bruesk directed. "I'm gonna get you some more mug shots."

"Hey, Joe. We got a recent shot of Donald Roch hanging around?" Bruesk asked the desk sergeant.

Caron looked up from his desk in the bull pen, "Hey boss, I hear Roch's working down at Libby's." A quick phone call confirmed it.

Ten days after her assault, Detective Bruesk drove Charlotte Jarrett over to Libby's Canning Plant to view Don Roch as he worked on the line. As they got closer to the plant Charlotte turned pale and her hands trembled.

"Don't worry, Mrs. Jarrett. I'm gonna be right by your side," Bruesk reassured her as he parked the squad car. She took his arm as they walked through the lot. He could feel her body shake. When her step wobbled he stopped to let her gain her composure.

"Ready?" he asked as they approached the cat walk that circled the line.

She nodded. They moved forward. Charlotte lifted her chin and looked down. Her eyes swept across the line.

"Take your time, Ma'am," Bruesk said. "They're working. Don't know we're here."

Charlotte Jarrett studied the men on the line. "He's not here," she sighed. "I wish he was. None of these men are him."

With her assailant still on the loose, Charlotte Jarrett no longer felt safe. She quit her waitress job and began seeing a psychiatrist on a weekly basis. Five long years passed before Charlotte got to attach a name to the face of her tormentor. Even after that, like a sleepless night, fear always pooled beneath the surface of her life.

20

Linda Wandrus November 6, 1950 — January 14, 1969

> I stole her key, and then later fifty-two cents. That's all.

David Torgerson moved up to Minneapolis so he could bum a ride or two over to Lino Lakes in order to see Lana on visiting days. She was released from Lino Lakes on the day she turned eighteen.

While waiting for her best friend Teresa at the Mesabi Nugget, Linda Wandrus glanced through the *Daily Journal*, laughingly called the daily urinal by true iron rangers. A cold wind swept across the diner when Terri Toor entered. By the time she removed her coat and slid into the bench across from Linda, the waitress appeared with their order, a plate of fries with the skins left on and a couple of cherry cokes. Terri fingered the size-ten 1968 Aurora-Hoyt Lakes high school ring dangling from a gold chain slung around her neck while Linda filled her in on her dating life in Minneapolis.

"So which one do you like best?" Terri asked Linda between sips of soda. Terri had only dated one guy her whole life, her high school sweetheart, Lyle, and she hoped he'd replace his class ring for a diamond this Christmas, which was just two weeks away.

"Well, John reminds me of Craig," Linda said, picking up a French fry smothered in ketchup. "You know, he's tall, sandy-haired, and has the same sky-blue eyes." Linda sighed as she thought about breaking up with her high school beau Craig, which had happened just before she moved to the Twin Cities. "He's a nice guy like Craig. John's quit working at the Bureau though," she said, pausing to reflect on the state of her affairs. "John says he doesn't want to be a stock boy his whole life. He's gonna enroll in college so I don't know, you know, how much I'll be seeing him and all."

"What about the other one?" Terri said leaning forward.

"Oh Bob. I just met him at my Uncle Charlie's party down in the city. Can't tell yet," Linda said, twisting a strand of her long hair around her index finger—a nervous habit she had picked up working as a clerk at the Bureau of Engraving. "He asked me to go out for pizza next week though so we'll see."

"You still living with your sister?"

"Gosh no. I moved the first of December over to Chicago Avenue." Linda reached for another fry from the plate the two girls shared. "Some creepy guy was bugging me at the bus stop and I wanted to get away from this married guy in our building too. A total jerk. I mean, I never knew he was married or nothing," she said rolling her eyes toward the ceiling.

"Huh?"

"Oh, this guy in my sister's building. Met him on the first day. He saw us carrying boxes and stuff into the apartment and offered to help. Kinda cute, you know. He had a ponytail," Linda said, feeling flames of scarlet hop-scotch up her slim neck.

"And?"

"He asked me over to his apartment a couple of times that kind of stuff. Then just like that 'poof' his wife showed up," Linda said snapping her fingers across her face. "Made me really mad, you know, I'd never go out with someone else's guy."

Terri nodded. Of course she knew that. Linda was a nice girl and trustworthy not carefree like her sister Dawn. Linda was more cautious and responsible, a true Finlander. Probably a good thing, Terri thought, lots of crime down there in the big city.

"Wow, it must be really great to have your own place," Terri said her voice filled with admiration.

"Yeah, so far I like it, "Linda admitted. "Stevie's gonna come stay with me over Christmas break. He says he misses having me kick around the house."

"That's so sweet. Wish I had a baby brother."

"Yeah, I'm lucky," Linda said with a smile.

Torgerson first saw her waiting at the bus stop downtown. She almost always caught the 5:22. He only had to nose around three times to figure out she worked at the Bureau of Engraving. Linda Wandrus' hair, the color and sheen of unshelled pecans, glinted in the fading sun. She was a petite woman with soft smoky-grey eyes, hair, parted down the middle, fell down past her shoulders. Snow fell. Bundled against the cold, most of the bus riders looked bone weary.

He pulled his ski cap down so it touched his eyebrows and slipped his wool scarf across the lower half of his face. She didn't notice him as he shuffled down the aisle past her seat to the bench in the back of the bus. Staring out the big back window, he saw her enter an apartment building on Chicago Avenue.

Over a slice of Vescio's sausage pizza, Linda figured out how Bob Evans came to be at her Uncle Charlie's party. They were second cousins. Still, as they left Dinky Town Linda decided to invite Bob to go with her to Mary Hanson's upcoming party.

"You'll like Mary," Linda said. "I mean, I do. We eat lunch together and everything down at the Bureau," Linda explained. "It's pot luck, but you don't have to bring nothing. I'm gonna make peanut butter rice crispy bars."

"What time should I pick you up?" Bob asked as he pulled up to the curb.

"It starts at five or so, I guess. Not far. She lives near Nokomis."

"How 'bout we get together before then?" Bob asked.

"Nah, I can't. My brother Steve is coming back with me right after Christmas. We're gonna bring in the New Year. He's riding back home with my sister that Friday so the fourth is the first time I'll be free."

Torgerson only had to wait outside her apartment building in the biting cold air a couple of times before she walked down the ice packed sidewalk. Turning his back on her, he crossed the street to gain full view of her apartment building. It was turning dark. After she went inside he looked up. In a couple of minutes the back corner unit of the top floor lit up. After stepping inside the foyer, he studied the fourth floor mail boxes: three guys, a Mr. and Mrs.' and one L. Wandrus. Not hard to figure out: women living alone always used just their first initial. He touched the handwritten label, which stood out from the others with their raised letters stamped across a blue stripe of plastic tape: 414.

"The party was neat," Linda told Mary over lunch. "What do you think about Bob?"

"He was Okay," Mary fudged. "You and John make a cuter couple though. What's he been up to?"

"I dunno, haven't heard from him," Linda said, as she blew on her steaming cream of potato soup.

"He'll call, you'll see. Give it time."

Linda looked up to Mary, trusted her opinion. She did like John better than Bob, that's for sure, but she had made another date with Bob for the day after tomorrow. "Oh, well, better get back to work. Better a grave mine than an iron mine," Linda joked.

As soon as she put in a year, the Bureau would reimburse for classes at the Affiliated Art School. She practiced drawing every night so she could get accepted. Who wouldn't want to get trained in a school where Charles Schultz had once taught? The phone was ringing as she unlocked her door after work that day. She dropped her groceries on the sofa and picked up.

"Linda? It's John. I was wondering if we could get together tonight. I bought you a little something for Christmas."

"Yeah, sure!" Linda said, happy. In her excitement, she forgot all about the date she had made with Bob, otherwise she would never have stood him up like that.

Phil and Roberta Brown took pride in how well they managed the apartment building at 420 Chicago Avenue. Roberta Brown had plenty to do what with a toddler and sixteen units. She placed the ads, showed and rented the units, cleaned the common halls, collected the weekly rent, and handled tenant complaints while Phil took care of the building maintenance.

Not so bad, Roberta thought, the free rent helped them make ends meet and she liked greeting the residents from her open office as they came and went about their business. The busy times were in the morning and late afternoon. Roberta was organized. She created forms for complaints or repairs and kept meticulous records of the weekly rent receipts as well as any petty cash expenditures.

The efficient office space, a small room attached to the back of the caretaking apartment, mirrored a hotel check-in. If she wasn't sitting at her desk, tenants could alert Roberta with a ring of the silver bell that sat on the top of the half wall. Because the bolt on the Dutch door that led to the lobby was too high for her active two year old to reach, Roberta felt secure in leaving her son, Timmy, on his own for a minute or two while she ducked into her apartment to get him a bottle or fix a quick snack. Sometimes Roberta opened the glass case that held the duplicate keys for each unit and grabbed a bunch of them for Timmy to play with. He loved to shake the keys.

As soon as her husband got home from his outside job, he checked in at the office. Now that the heating season was on them, complaints about faulty radiators were a given. "Four-twelve says his bedroom radiator's leaking," Roberta reported as she handed Phil the unit's pass key.

"I'm on it," Phil said, tightening his worn leather tool belt, "might as well check the whole floor out while I'm there. Give me the rest of the fourth floor keys why donncha."

Roberta plucked four more keys off their respective hooks. "Four-fourteen's not here," she muttered. "I gave Timmy a bunch of them this morning. I'll look around. Just knock on her door," Roberta instructed her husband. "Remember her? She's the quiet new girl, Linda."

After fixing the leaking radiator in 412, Phil Brown knocked on Linda Wandrus' door.

"Who is it?"

"Caretaker, Miss. I'm here to check your radiators."

"Tell me your name, please," Linda said, remembering her mother's warning about not opening her door to strangers.

"Phil Brown, Roberta's husband," Phil responded patiently.

Linda flipped the door's lock before opening her door a crack so she could peek outside. Respecting her caution, Phil stepped back so she could see him fully.

"Oh, hi. I'm sorry. Come on in Mr. Brown." Linda said apologetically, "My mom tells me to make sure and all, you know."

"That's Okay. I understand. Good to trust your mother," Phil grinned. "Can't be too careful that's what I always say."

He heard a jingle-jangle coming from the office in the corner and spied a little boy playing all alone with a pile of keys. Quick as a rabbit, He checked out the numbers above the hooks in the open cabinet on the far wall. Slipping the bolt on the split door, he lifted the latch and took three steps before reaching up to snag the keys to 414. All in less than a minute. "Not bad, not bad," he congratulated himself.

Loose snow swirled outside Bauberg's corner grocery. Not quite mid-January and the ruts cut a foot deep on either side of ice-packed side streets. The city made a lot of money fining folks for parking on the wrong side of the street, winter wasn't Bauberg's best season. From his perch behind the cash register Bill Bauberg saw the tiny teen walking his way. Even with three layers piled on, Bauberg judged she wouldn't push the scale into triple digits. The bells jiggled as she opened the heavy door and stepped inside.

"Cold enuf fer ya?" Bauberg kidded.

Linda grinned. "This ain't nothin'. You know I come from the Mesabi Iron Range. Embarrass is always on the morning news as the coldest town in the nation. Gives us bragging rights," she said over her shoulder as she walked down the aisle.

"Help yourself to a cookie from the jar," Bauberg invited as he rang up Linda's order. "Hey, woudja look it that. Comes to $2.22," he laughed. "You a poker player, kid? This'd be a good hand if you were."

The next morning Linda stopped by the office to pay her bi-monthly rent. "I'm a little short," Linda apologized as she handed Mrs. Brown thirty dollars. "I'll have the rest of it on Friday. Any chance I could move to something smaller on the first?"

"Nothing's opened up yet, dear. People don't like to move in the middle of the winter. Come March things will loosen up. I'll letcha know soon's that happens," Roberta patted Linda's hand. "Hey, by the way, somehow I misplaced the pass key for your apartment. Can you be a dear and get a duplicate made? Just bring the receipt and I'll reimburse you from petty cash. Okay?"

That evening Linda gave Mrs. Brown the requested duplicate key along with the receipt for fifty-two cents.

"Here you go, sweetie," Roberta said handing over two quarters and two pennies.

After Linda failed to show-up at work the next day, Mary Bovee skipped lunch to drive over to her friend's apartment.

"It's a good thing Linda made me that duplicate," Roberta said as she escorted Mary to the fourth floor. "Dependable, and quiet. I could use more tenants like her."

The two women froze when they saw the partially clothed body submerged in the claw foot tub. While Mrs. Brown ran to the phone, Mary rushed to the tub. She knelt, placed her arm behind Linda's stiff shoulders raising her above the water. Mary cradled Linda's head and gently brushed her friend's long brown hair off her face before reaching down to pull the plug.

A slew of detectives converged on the scene. Jones and Conroy of Minneapolis Squad 118 arrived first. Bureau of Identification Officers Boike and Nelson showed up next. Officers Blanch, Whalen, Pufahl, Andersen, Matthews and Johnson added to the congestion in apartment 414. Detective Shoemacher strolled in right after Homicide Detective Hansey. Twenty-eight years on the job had turned Hansey's hair white. He'd walked through the cesspool of crime the city had to offer but dead girls could still make his heart drop a notch or too.

"Christ, would you look at that Shoemacher? She's just a baby, for God's sake," Hansey groaned as they stared at the petite, white female lying at the bottom of the bathtub. Her legs were flexed, her head rested under the faucet. Blood and white foam flowed from her nostrils and her mouth. Although the body was clothed from the waist down, the elastic of the panty hose was bunched up below the victim's waistline. A black bra had been pulled up fully exposing her breasts. One sleeve of the brown jersey sweater had been tied and knotted around her neck.

"Yeah, glad you caught this one pal," Shoemacher said, with a flat tone. "If this ain't the boyfriend, this one's gonna bite you in the ass."

Hansey gave orders. "Jones, you and Conroy take the building's first two floors, Pufahl, Andersen, three and four. Boike and Nelson you know what to do—document the scene here while Shoemacher writes it up. Blanch get downstairs. Hold the landlady's hand till I get there. Whalen you do the same with the other witness. Anyone left over—set up the tape outside, walk the alleys. If you're staying in, glove-up. Johnson, call this shit into the station. Have 'em get the medical examiner out here on the double. Everyone reports to me. Got it?"

When the medical examiner removed Linda Wandrus' body from the tub, he noticed a bruise on the top of her right shoulder and a small bruise on the rear left side of her head. "We'll know more after the autopsy," Dr. Coe promised Hansey. "Come by around five o'clock. I'll have her done."

Hansey was late, quarter of six. The M.E. sat in his office shuffling paperwork. "Hey, Doc, how's it going?"

The M.E. nodded, "Hansey, take a seat. Got her file right here. I'll get my girl to type it up and make a copy for you tomorrow."

"Yup, that'll work. So bring me up to speed. What'd you find?"

"White, female, nineteen, five foot two, 102 pounds. Petechial hemorrhaging on her face and on the inside of her eyelids indicates probable strangulation. I took a blood sample from the heart just to make sure she didn't die from drowning. I found a partial plate lodged in the back of her throat so I removed her larynx. Fractured cortical cartilage, fractured hyoid, and hemorrhages in the strap muscles of the neck. Looks like manual strangulation to me. Musta had dinner. Found creamed peas in the stomach."

"How about drugs, alcohol?"

"Nope. Clean."

"Raped?"

"Vaginal semen but I don't think so. Not pregnant."

Dr. Coe gave Hansey the victim's dried out clothing. Each piece—dark brown panty hose, black lace panties, brown skirt, black brassiere, and a pullover brown jersey blouse—had been bagged and tagged.

The next night Hansey reviewed all of the reports his men had submitted. He started with Shoemacher's summary of the bedroom: I noticed at the foot of the bed a brown purse, closed, and also a coin purse and a wallet. Also, a small white box, tipped upside down, which had contained sewing needles. A search of the purse and coin purse and wallet revealed no money; in fact, in a search of the entire apartment, we found only one penny.

"Hhmm, where's the fifty-two cents she got from the landlady?" Hansey pondered before reading more of Shoemacher's report, which stated: there was also a green jumper and a pink nightgown lying on the bed; near the head of the bed were some sketching pads and a box of pencils and crayon; the sheet was rumpled, but not unusually so; some pieces of a rubber eraser were found next to the pillow; under the bed was a pair of house slippers and a pair of shoes. The victim spent some time lying in bed, drawing pictures, Hansey decided.

Turning to the crime scene photos, Hansey studied one taken inside of the entry into the apartment. It showed two impressions at the top of the door frame. The next picture showed a butter knife lying on the floor, about ten feet away from the door. Looks like she took extra precautions when she was home, Hansey surmised. His wife had done that—put butter knifes in the door frame when the kids were little so, even if they could work the lock, they still wouldn't be able to open the door at night. Made her sleep easy.

He knew from his conversation with the landlady the Wandrus teenager didn't open her door to strangers. These pictures suggested she hadn't let someone in. A guy would have to push a door pretty hard to dislodge a knife like that, Hansey concluded. Made him think some more about the missing key. He had already checked to see if he could reach the keys by reaching across the open doorway. No go. A guy would have to step inside the office to grab them.

Boike's report categorized the evidence from the scene. Latent finger prints. Check. Bagged bed sheet—Hansey made a note to have it examined for semen stains. Cigarettes, lots of them: two king-sized Winston filtered cigarette butts, found outside the apartment door; ten Pall Mall cigarettes, smoked halfway, and one Camel cigarette butt. All of them were found inside the ashtray. Hansey scratched his head, huh, the girl didn't smoke. He wondered: did she have a party? Didn't seem like the party-girl type.

The police background check of the residents in the Chicago Avenue apartment building revealed ten tenants (out of sixteen units) had some sort of criminal record. The charges included: non-support, drunkenness, petty larceny, contributing to the delinquency of a minor, robbery, burglary and, the most serious offense, second degree assault.

Never know who is livin' next door, Hansey grumbled to himself as he compiled a list of suspects. Past boyfriends; relatives, which included an uncle with a long criminal record and a shiftless brother-in-law; apartment building tenants; work mates; and known sex offenders living in the neighborhood. Of course, he'd have to drive up to the Iron Range to interview her family and friends. Hansey knew he faced miles to go before he slept. Take the Scenic Byway, he told himself, see a little of Superior's forest.

Linda's uncle Chet contacted the detectives working the Wandrus' case on more than one occasion to share his suspicions about two family members: Dawn Wandrus' new husband, Gayland Pyle, and his nieces' other uncle, George Evans. Detective Hansey followed up on both leads. Neither one panned out. After interviewing and carefully checking out their alibis Hansey also crossed two of the boyfriends, John Steel and Bob Evans, off his list.

"Looks like Shoemacher was right, this one's gonna take time," Hansey considered. He knew the longer it took the more likely a case would run cold. Hansey didn't want to shove this one into the phantom backpack of unsolved cases he carried around with him long after other cops would have let go of 'em. "Looney's come outta the woodwork in a case like this," he muttered to himself.

Hearing of Linda Wandrus' death, Louise Armstrong called Detective Hansey. "My husband Jim worked with that dead girl up there at the Bureau of Engraving. I can put two and two together. You betcha, I can," she huffed. Mrs. Armstrong theorized her husband killed Wandrus because: he lived four blocks from Linda's previous address, worked with her, and had an explosive nature, having stabbed his wife in the chest during a domestic. "This whole damn thing pushed me over the edge that's why I'm in the psych ward down at Hennepin," she said, exhaling audibly. Hansey knew he couldn't crack this case that easy. It only took him a minute to get Armstrong to admit her husband had been home for the entire evening on the date of the murder.

Ronald Joseph Dodge, also known as 'Pony,' was easy to find with a quick record search. He was sitting out a forty-five day term for disorderly conduct. On January 31, Hansey and Pufahl took a road trip to Blue Earth County jail, a hundred miles southwest of the cities. Dodge greeted them calmly until they said they wanted to talk about the Wandrus murder.

"What the hell you guys talkin' to me fer?" Pony boy shouted. "I ain't no God damn killer!"

"We just gotta clear this up, Ron," Hansey soothed. "Her sister says you guys dated back in October."

"Yeah, that's right. Linda didn't have many friends in the cities, so we kinda' hung out," Dodge admitted. "Her place mostly. We had sex there twice," Dodge confided, "but come November she don't want nothing more to do with me."

"How come?" Detective Hansey asked.

"Well, uhmm, me and my old lady, Adele, we were on-again-off-again, see. I guess she figured out I was married," Dodge confessed.

"Go figure," Pufahl smirked.

"Ron, do you have an alibi for January fourteen?" Hansey probed.

"Let me see. Yeah, that was the weekend Adele…she kicked me out again. I was pretty wasted after that. For about a week, I think. I stayed in an apartment building on Aldrich with uh, a Diane and Karen, their place, you know.

Then I moved in with a Kathy and Sherry, same building. They oughtta remember me," Dodge bragged.

"Looks like we stumbled across a 'true ladies' man,'" Pufahl muttered loud enough to be heard down the cell block.

"Look, man, I'll do whatever you need," Dodge exclaimed. "I ain't got nothin' to hide here. You gotta believe me."

After making a full set of his palm prints the detectives returned to the cities. Six months later Hansey officially crossed Dodge off his list when the prints didn't match any of those found at the crime scene. Linda Wandrus' death was officially classified as a homicide on January 24, 1969. The form listed the primary cause of death as asphyxia due to ligature and manual strangulation. The investigation into her death, active for one year, would remain unsolved for another four years.

At the end of February, 1969, Lana Iverson and David Torgerson took off to visit Susie, Lana's sister, and her husband, Bruce, who was stationed in Texas. After Bruce's unit was called up in June, Torgerson drove the Iverson sisters back to Rochester.

"Me and David got married down in Texas, the beginning of March," Lana announced to her mother on the day they arrived home.

"Funny, this is the first I heard about it," Darlene said. "You got a marriage license?"

"Yup," Lana said, digging around in her purse. "I can't find it—must be out in the car somewheres. I'll show you later, after me and David get settled. We had a real fun trip. 'bout half way we got real low on money. David, he come up with a great idea. See what we did was, coming into a town, we scoped out the churches. David picked one," Lana said with a big grin. "When the minister come to the door, David, he says real sad like, 'We're traveling to see a sick aunt and run out of gas money.' Worked every time, didn't it, Susie?"

David liked it when she bragged on him that way, made him feel like a man. Lana almost always thought he was pretty funny too. The first time he met her sister, Janice, he grabbed for her boobs and Lana laughed real loud before saying, "Wait just a sec, let me fine the camera. I gotta git a shot a this one!"

David liked big boobs. Both of Lana's sisters had nice knockers. He didn't mess round with Susie's no more though. Nobody messed with Susie twice. One time when he reached out and pinched her nipple Susie said, "You cut that shit out or I'll knock your block off, asshole."

Then he stuffed his hands into his pants pockets, walked away real quick.

Janice Carlson was glad to have her sisters back in Rochester but she wasn't crazy about Torgerson. She complained on the phone to her husband, Ronald, "David, he tries to put on a nice show saying, 'Lana, honey, do you want me to get you something, honey?' Honey this and honey that—lookin' at her with them moon eyes—makes me want to puke."

Decades later, Janice Carlson still shed hard tears over the loss of her oldest sister, Lana.

21

Julie Merhman April 12, 1950—July 13, 1969

> I took the belt, the one that went with her blouse. That was it.

"Who wants chocolate?" Julie asked holding a half pound of Hersey's Kisses above her head.

"I do, I do," her sisters, Diane and Kathy clamored.

"How 'bout you, Loupot?" Julie said to Cindy, the baby of the Merhman clan, as she ripped open the cellophane bag spilling a few pieces on the kitchen table. Eager hands reached forward, but Julie's was faster. "You gotta earn 'em first," she declared cupping the kisses in her palm.

Diane, just three years younger than Julie, cast a suspicious eye. "What we gotta do? I'm not taking your turn at dishes!"

"Nope, this won't be hard. Just stick your nose in my armpit and take a big whiff," Julie explained. "Course, you should know I just got back from band practice and my sweater is pretty stinky. Think you can handle it?"

Julie raised one arm and all three of her sisters passed their noses through and then, as promised, she rewarded them with a shower of foil kisses. Loupot giggled with delight as her big sister, whom she called 'Ju-Ju,' hugged her.

"How are the Bluebirds, Loupot? Tweet, Tweet," Julie teased before adding, "Next time, you'll have to sip Tabasco sauce."

They all laughed. The second of six children, Julie liked to make up silly rules for her younger sisters to follow. Before Julie left home after graduating high school, Loupot watched her every move, following her around the house like a swooning puppy. She sat next to Ju-Ju as she drew chic fashion models, like those found on the front of Butterick sewing pattern envelopes, or quirky poses of 'Mr. Pitiful,' an imaginary character Julie had created.

Loupot noticed how her big sister crossed her legs at the knee, so lady-like, and copied it. Pursing her lips, the little girl pretended to apply lipstick just like Julie did. She wanted to grow up to be beautiful, poised, and talented, too. Loupot had just turned seven when her playful big sister, Ju-Ju, was found dead, and then her childhood melted away with the July heat.

Julie Merhman's friendship with Amy Stevens started during their freshman year at Osseo High. In the 1960's, Osseo was a small community with little racial diversity other than the heritage of its name, taken from the Native American name Waseia, Osseo translates to: there is light.

Osseo's citizens prized their high school marching band almost as much as they did their football team and its scruffy Osseo Oriole mascot. Everyone in town turned out for the Lions Roar: a street fair with crafts, a parking lot carnival, and a parade starting at Sipe's Park that ended at the high school.

While twirling her aluminum baton, Julie high-stepped the parade route with the rest of the majorettes. She looked good in the orange and black dance costume with its flirty satin skirt and the flame tassels that dangled from her white calf-high boots. The crowd cheered each time she caught her aluminum baton after sending it sky-high. When she missed, Julie made a graceful dip and came back up smiling to scattered applause. Julie's mother, Winifred, attended every one of her performances.

After graduating from high school in 1968, Julie and Amy moved to St. Cloud, located sixty miles north of the Twin Cities. Although it would still be considered small by most standards, St. Cloud was twenty times larger than Osseo. Julie found work as a nursing home aide while Amy trained to become a beautician. Being a university town, St. Cloud offered plenty of night life for a pretty, petite brunette with a laugh as infectious and exuberant as a Sousa March.

Julie attracted two earnest suitors: Guy Carlson and Ray Garcia. If they ever needed a poster boy, clean-shaven, Guy Carlson could have posed for a Burma Shave advertisement. He treated everyone he met with quiet respect, which is why Amy liked him better than Ray; but it was Ray who stole Julie's heart. Garcia's family had migrated from San Antonio, which might account for his Marlboro Man allure; even though Ray never saddled up, having been born and raised in the heart of Minneapolis.

After Amy earned her cosmetology license both girls returned home. Julie found work as a dietary aide at Fairview Hospital in South Minneapolis and socked away her paychecks so she could move closer to work and to Ray, who had moved back into his parents' home in South Minneapolis. By the end of June, Julie's bank account tallied two hundred dollars, enough for a security deposit and first month's rent. Scouring the Sunday edition of the *Minneapolis Tribune*, she found a listing for an efficiency apartment not far from work. She set up a meeting with the building owner, Larry Lecher, after her hospital shift ended on Monday, July 7, 1969.

"So do the day-bed and the kitchen table stay?" Julie asked as she surveyed the first floor two-room apartment on East Twenty-Fifth Street.

"Yeah. The paint's fresh too. Oven's been cleaned. Good refrigerator here," Lecher pointed out as Julie opened a kitchen cabinet. "You lookin' to rent this month? I can give a pretty good deal if ya are."

"Really?"

"You employed, right?"

"Uh, huh. I work at Fairview Hospital. Before that I worked at a nursing home in St. Cloud."

"That's hard work. Must tense up your neck and shoulders," Lecher said. "I'm a professional masseuse, you know. Can't really work those kinks out over clothes though," he said. Pausing, he shifted his eyes to the floor. "You'd have to strip, at least down to the waist," he added, shrugging his shoulders to indicate this was no big deal. He swiped one hand through his bangs and extended the other, palm up. "First massage is a freebie. See how you like it."

"Ahh, no thanks," Julie replied, taking a step back. "What did you say the rent was?"

"Normally, runs seventy-five a month. But you can have the rest of July for thirty-five if you want. Deposit same as rent."

"That sounds good. I'll take it," Julie said. "Is a check Okay?"

"Yes ma'am, just complete this paper work right here. I'll get you the key. My phone number's posted near the mail boxes in case you need repairs or anything. I just live ten minutes away," Lecher said, flashing a toothy grin. "Massage offer's good any time you want now."

Julie's dad, Gary, and brother, Mark, helped her move in on the following Saturday. Ray Garcia was waiting at the apartment when they pulled up. She didn't bring much furniture: a roll-away cot, dresser, stuffed chair, TV, and a couple of end tables filled up the small space. After loading the refrigerator with beer, Ray gave Mark a hand with the big stuff while Julie and her dad scurried back and forth carrying household boxes and her hanging clothes.

Hot and sweaty, they all enjoyed a cold one after the truck was emptied. Julie's dad planted a kiss on her forehead and said his goodbye's leaving the young couple alone to unpack. That evening Julie and Ray ate a pepperoni and green olive pizza, delivered from Uptown's Leaning Tower of Pizza, and drank beer while watching a late night movie. Later, they opened up the day bed and shoved it next to the roll-away cot. Ray stayed the night.

Torgerson was looking for work again. After hitch-hiking to the Twin Cities, he took a room at the YMCA in South Minneapolis. He always got itchy around his birthday, which was only three days away. Even at ten o'clock in the evening his sleeping room felt hot and damp. His shoes scuffed across the cement sidewalk as he headed up Blaisdell Avenue. Three minutes later he turned right onto Lake Street filled with neon signs and liquor stores that had metal screens across the plate glass to protect the merchandise. He peered into a couple of dive bars on either side of the 35W underpass but decided they were too noisy and crowded, so he walked on. He turned up Portland Avenue because there were houses and apartment buildings with tree-lined boulevards. He'd only been hoofing it for half-an-hour before he saw her through the window of a first floor apartment on the corner of Portland and Twenty-fifth. She must be short, he decided, otherwise how could she curl herself into the window sill like that.

> Petite, petite's good. Nice hair too—long.

Her head was tipped down so that her hair, the color of bourbon, scraped across the tablet she was holding.

"Who you writing to?"

"A friend from high school," Julie said. She looked up and smiled. "She's in Brainerd now, going to school. You live around here?"

"Not far. I use to live in Rochester. Only been here for a week. Don't know nobody here though. I just started walking to cool off, see the neighborhood and stuff," Torgerson said, looking straight into her warm brown eyes. "That beer you're drinking sure looks good. You wouldn't happen to have another?"

She said, "Sure."

Torgerson settled down with a few more beers until dawn come up over the building tops.

The phone rang in the Mehrman household shortly after 10:00 a.m. on Tuesday, July 15. Julie's shift supervisor told Winifred her daughter had not reported for work on Monday or for today's seven a.m. shift.

"Oh, goodness, this isn't like Julie," Winifred Mehrman replied. "She must be very sick. She moved over the weekend and her phone hasn't been hooked up yet. Thanks for letting me know. I'll get back to you as soon as find out how she is." Worried, Winifred phoned Ray Garcia to find out if he knew why Julie had not shown up for work.

"I haven't seen her since Sunday," Ray said, shock registering in his voice. "I'll go check on her right now, Mrs. Mehrman, no problem."

"That's good. Thanks, Ray. I'm going to call Laura to see if she can drive over with me. I'll see you soon."

Ray showed up at Julie's place in record time. When she did not answer her door, even after he yelled out her name, he bounded up the stairs to get the landlady. After hearing Garcia out, Mrs. Mattson grabbed her duplicate key and hurried over to apartment number one with him.

She knocked three times.

They waited.

She knocked again.

Silence.

Mrs. Mattson put the key into the lock and pushed the door open calling out, "Miss Mehrman—Julie?"

As they stepped through the front door of the apartment, Julie's nude body, her bare feet facing them, legs spread wide, stunned them both. The color drained from Ray's face as he started toward her lifeless form. "Stop, stay back," Mrs. Mattson commanded as she rushed past him. She grabbed a throw rug from the floor and covered Julie's torso. She didn't want anyone else to see the young woman exposed like that. It wouldn't be right.

Minneapolis Squad 551 received a call from Mrs. Mattson of 602 East 25th Street, at 10:57 a.m. on July 15, 1969. Officers Larson and Welters responded. Let into apartment 1, by Mrs. Mattson, they saw the body of a young woman lying in the middle of the roll-a-way bed—a pink scatter rug covered her naked torso. Julie Mae Merhman had spent just two days and two nights in her very own, first-place.

Larson threw open the windows as Welter pulled the rug off Julie's corpse. The officers saw a bite mark on the teenager's right breast, near the nipple. Welter stepped closer and stared at her bloated face. Anyone could tell the girl had been dead for some time. Her blackened tongue stuck out and drops of dried blood caked her indigo lips. A faint bruise dotted the left side of her neck. Looking at his partner, Welter pointed to what looked like a splotch of rust on the sheet next to her ear. "Yah, I'll get that," Larson nodded.

Having been notified of a DOA, Detective Shoemacher and Captain Johnson arrived at 11:10 a.m. Detective Shoemacher, a burly six-footer, had broken-up more than his share of barroom brawls over on Hennepin Avenue, the hub of Minneapolis nightlife. He had a three-inch scar just above his right eyebrow, from a broken beer bottle brandished by some low-life, to prove it. That's a cop's lot, nothing but low-life's especially for the night-time beat cop. Thank God I made detective a decade ago, Shoemacher reflected. He still dealt with the scum of the earth, but it wasn't so up-close-and-personal. Being a detective was a lot better than patrol.

"I ain't no virgin," Shoemacher thought as he reached over to pop his glove compartment. He removed the economy-sized jar of Vicks he kept there for scenes like this one and slapped a gob of it under his nostrils. As the lead investigator, it was up to him to close this case and he wanted to do it fast. Shoemacher called in Officers Cich and Benson to document the scene. Cich made a quick sketch of the two-room efficiency apartment while Benson shot a roll of film. Cich's simple drawing showed the day bed flat against the wall and the roll-a-way cot center-stage. A yellow slash-mark indicated the victim's remains.

While the coroner's van hauled the deceased girl away, Shoemacher motioned to the clothing strewn across the floor of the efficiency, "Bag those clothes up, boys." Welters and Larson, the first officers on the scene, placed a brassiere, rolled up panties, a multi-colored top, and a pair of white shorts, torn just below the zipper, inside a clear, plastic envelop. Before they scooped it up, Benson snapped a shot of the blood stained pillowslip hanging in plain view on the back of an over-stuffed chair. The duty officers also inventoried all of the bedding before they gathered it up to send onto the lab. Shoemacher noticed a beer can sitting on a table next to the cot as he followed Captain Johnson into the kitchen. Surveying the room, he spied a box sitting next to the garbage can filled to the brim with a couple dozen empty beer cans.

"Christ, that's a lot a beer." Shoemacher whistled. "You think she's legal?" he asked before adding, "Bet the burrito brought it over."

"Guess she was still alive Sunday night," Johnson replied holding up a three-page letter, written in girlish script and dated 10 p.m. July 13.

"I'm going out to talk with the boyfriend," Shoemacher sighed. "After you finish up in here, come join me."

"Detective Shoemacher," Shoemacher said, stretching his beefy hand out to Ray Garcia, who stood ashen-faced in the bright sunshine just outside the yellow tape. "The land lady said you two found the victim. She says she was your girlfriend. That right?"

Ray nodded.

"You'll have to go down to the precinct fill out some paper work with Captain Johnson soon as he comes out," Shoemacher explained. "Alright if I ask you a couple a questions now?

"Yeah, sure," Ray mumbled.

How long have you known Miss Merhman? "

"We met last year. Up in Saint Cloud."

"You saw her last… ?"

"Saturday. Saturday night I stayed over. She just moved in, ah…"

"You had sexual relations." Shoemacher stated rather than asked.

"Yeah, we made love three times Saturday night," Ray replied candidly. "Once, before we went to sleep, then again in the middle of the night, and in the morning. I left around five o'clock, Sunday night."

The beer cans and the south-of-the border boyfriend bothered Detective Shoemacher. He stood there trying to remember the last time he screwed some broad even once and here's this Mexican hat dance goin' at it like a frigging rabbit. That really pissed him off. He didn't think much of the girl's housekeeping either. No class he decided, shaking it off. Maybe job burn-out or too many cases had hardened him. It happens.

"Was there a fight or anything?" Shoemacher asked, cocking his scarred eye-brow.

"No. We were happy, she was happy. Had a new job, apartment, me… ," Ray's voice trailed off.

"So Ray, you'd be willing to take a lie detector test then," Shoemacher said as he walked Garcia over to Captain Johnson's squad car. "I mean you got nothing to hide, right?"

While Julie's sister-in-law, Laurel, drove her mother, Winifred, across town the Merhman household phone rang. Kathy Merhman, then fifteen, said "Hello?" after picking up on the third ring. "This is the Minneapolis police department," a bland male voice announced. "I am calling to report that Julie Merhman has been found dead." Kathy dropped the receiver and bolted out the front door. She sank into the green grass, curled her legs, and rolled across the yard.

"She's dead, she's dead, Julie's dead," she screamed for the world to hear.

As soon as Laurel pulled over to the Portland Avenue curb, Winifred noticed the bright yellow and black warning tape that cordoned off the entrance to Julie's first floor efficiency. Taking the plastic streamer as a sign that Julie was highly contagious, Mrs. Merhman hurried to the apartment entrance and saw a phone number posted on Julie's front door. Pulling a pad and pen from her purse, Mrs. Merhman jotted the number down and then rushed toward the next door to ask if she might use the phone, which is when Mrs. Mattson, the landlady, stepped into her path.

"That poor girl…she was just lying there—dead," Mrs. Mattson blubbered, pointing at Julie's apartment door.

"You don't know what you're talking about," Mrs. Merhman insisted, her hands shaking as she pushed the crumpled phone number into Laurel's hand, gesturing for her to go make the phone call.

Winifred's knees buckled when Laurel returned to tell her the police had requested they drive to the Hennepin County Morgue in order to make a positive identification of Julie's body. Wrapping her thin arms around her mother-in-law, Laurel managed to get Winifred back to the car. They were both too numb to speak. Winifred handed over the keys and then stared straight ahead for the fifteen minute ride downtown.

After Winifred Mehrman identified her daughter's body for the morgue officials, she sat at Julie's side, stroking her silky brown hair. Memories of tap dancing recitals and the day Julie won her last baton-twirling trophy floated in space. Patting her baby's hand Winifred couldn't help but notice Julie's bruised arms. Detective Shoemacher talked with Mrs. Merhman at the coroner's office before she and Laurel drove home.

Given Winifred's deep love for her daughter, Detective Shoemacher's written account of their discussion is as mystifying as a Rorschach Ink blot. He wrote the following summary into this official report later that night: I talked with Mrs. Donald Merhman at Morgue. She stated the victim was a typical girl, apparently quite lazy, and not too neat in her personal habits. She knew of no drug addiction but stated her daughter did like to drink beer. She stated she met victim's boyfriend, Ray Garcia, and knew of no difficulty between them.

Shoemacher never followed-up with the Merhman family after this interview. He did, however, question Ray Garcia again. At the end of their second meeting, he escorted Garcia to the hospital and watched while blood and pubic hair samples were collected. After Ray's mother confirmed her only child had spent that Sunday evening at home, Shoemacher dismissed him as a suspect.

Shoemacher read Cich's hand-printed footnote later that day. It said: the screens on the French doors leading to the attached porch off the kitchen are in-place and intact. So it wasn't an intruder, Shoemacher said to himself.

Having learned about the apartment building owner's offer to give Julie a massage, Shoemacher added him to his persons-of-interest list.

Their interview was brief.

"I never ever touched her, Detective," Lecher declared, after admitting he had offered Julie a free massage. "You gotta believe me!"

"You got a key?"

"Uh, uh, no surr-ie-Bob," Lecher said. "The last gal—she, she replaced the lock. There are only two keys. Mrs. Mattson gave one to Miss Merhman and kept the other for herself."

"We're gonna need your cooperation here," Shoemacher said. "You willing to give a blood sample?"

"Sure, sure officer," Lecher said agreeably. "Anything you need. You got it."

Shoemacher wrote him off even before he fired-up his royal blue Crown Vic. Just another old fart trying to get laid, he thought to himself while jotting this summary into his field notes: It appears to me that Mr. Lecher, who owns several apartment houses, and rents mostly to women, considers himself quite a ladies' man. And his offer of a massage, apparently, is a method he uses to become acquainted with various women.

Two weeks after Julie's death, Shoemacher met with Julie Merhman's former Saint Cloud roomie, Amy Stevens. They chatted while Amy was between customers at J.C. Penney's Beauty Shop in Brookdale Shopping Center. Shoemacher's eyes watered from the stench of ammonia mixed with hair spray. This place smells worse than cat piss, he thought to himself. Why the hell do women put shit like this in their hair?

Shoemacher solicited information on Julie's character from Amy, who, according to his field notes described Julie as, "flighty, someone who threw her clothes on the floor, and liked to sleep in her underwear."

The standard line—healthy and did not use narcotics—showed up in Shoemacher's summary report of their talk too. Amy told Shoemacher that Julie dated two men when they lived together in Saint Cloud. Besides Garcia, she went out with a guy named Guy Carlson. Now Shoemacher had to follow-up with this Carlson fellow too. He phoned Carlson from the station house that same day.

"Guy," Shoemacher said, most times he liked to call subjects by their first name, "this is Detective Joseph Shoemacher, from the Fifth Precinct. I have a couple questions to ask you about Julie Merhman. I heard you and she dated some."

"Yes, sir."

"When was the last time you saw Miss Merhman?"

"Well, I stopped by her new apartment the Saturday before last," Guy replied. "I knew she moved in the Friday before and I wanted to say 'hi' and see the place, you know."

"Uh, huh," Shoemacher said.

"I bumped into Mr. Lecher, the building owner," the kid continued. "He was cleaning out her place so I asked him where Julie was. He said she didn't live there anymore and shut the door in my face. When I got home, I called Julie's mom. That's how I learned she was dead." Guy gulped, "Her mom told me they buried her in Weaver Lake Cemetery."

"Can you tell me where you were on July 13?" Shoemacher asked.

"I was at my sister's lake place up near Bemidji. I drove up after work on Friday and came back late Sunday night.

She lives in Maplewood, sir," Guy responded. "You can call her if you want. Her number is 555-1587."

Shoemacher never bothered to check Carlson's alibi. In the end, four scant pages comprised his entire investigative report. With the graphic nature of Julie Merhman's crime scene, it is hard to fathom the corner's conclusion listed on her death certificate: **cause of death—probable natural causes**. Given such short-shrift and lack of follow-up, the details of Julie Merhman's death disappeared like a whisper of morning fog.

22

Rebecca Hanson October 9, 1950–January 9, 1970

> I took the brown suede mini skirt—for Lana.

The front door bells jingled and a gust of December air blew around the counter every time a customer entered Dison's Drycleaners just off Broadway. Becky Hanson was dropping off some blue uniforms to be laundered and starched. He recognized them: Mayo Clinic blues and listened as she gave her address to the clerk. Fourth Avenue, she'd said. David Torgerson watched the clerk pin the information card to the pile of dirty wash before setting it inside the canvas bin.

Mild Minnesota winter days are like a good apple crisp and slightly tart. Rebecca Hanson buttoned up her coat before she left the drycleaner's to take the five-minute walk back to her job in medical records on the fifth floor of the clinic. Her sister, Bonnie (who worked as a nurse in obstetrics) helped Becky get the Mayo interview. Becky had met with her boss that morning to discuss her job performance; the six month anniversary came with a pay raise and health care coverage. Tonight they would celebrate. Becky's treat.

Torgerson finished mopping the floor and emptying the trash by the mid-afternoon lull. His head throbbed.

> Two lousy bucks an hour. Assholes at St. Mary's. Everybody's late. Lana's fun—a good kisser.

Finally, he spied it: Rebecca Hanson, 421 Fourth Avenue, 555-2132. He wrote it down on one of the counter forms and crammed it into his pocket before going outside to empty the trash. No one saw.

Becky took the tunnel to drop off the last bundle of charts from radiology. She clocked out a little after three before grabbing the phone to dial obstetrics. "Bonnie Hanson, please," she said, then waited for her sister's smooth voice, the efficient tone she used at work, to come on the line. "Hey, Bonnie, I got my raise today!" Becky exclaimed. "Meet me out front and we'll head over to Broadway and get one of those juicy burgers to celebrate."

"We got a baby coming, David. You're gonna be a father soon," Lana laughed patting her swollen tummy as she tore open the twin pack of Twinkies he had set on the table. She saw David puff out his chest. The baby was due in a couple weeks—by Christmas. He felt like a man.

In Lanesboro, a rural southeastern Minnesota community of fewer than 800 people, the Hanson's were upstanding, hard-working, church-going citizens. Their dairy farm, one-hundred-fifty head, sat in the heart of Fillmore County's rolling bluffs. The perfume of balsam joined with hot bread from the oven as Becky and Bonnie entered their mother's kitchen on Christmas Day. Bonnie hugged her mom, who was standing guard at the stove next to the kitchen sink and noticed the frost, which had spread and cracked like a delicate spider web halfway up the window. Their mother stirred her Christmas potato soup laden with apple smoked bacon and gobs of cheddar cheese. Homemade apple pies, baskets of cookies, and a plate of fudge sat on the kitchen counter in the crowded farm house.

Racing to the stairwell Becky shouted up the stairs, "We're home!" and then the sound of rapid footfalls tumbled down the stairs.

"I can't believe it. I missed you so much!" Pam screeched, grabbing Becky by the shoulders, dancing her about the room.

"Girls, girls," their mother laughed, "for heaven's sake, settle down."

"I got your letter yesterday," Pam bubbled. "Boy, Rochester sure sounds fun."

"It'll be even better when you come to live with us next year," Becky said, drawing her sister close. Only a year apart, growing up they had shared a bed along with their girlish dreams. With ten children in the family, the Hanson's had always drawn names for holiday gift giving but every year Becky bought something small for Pam.

Becky loved Christmas—all the noise and confusion as the whole family came together, the holiday lights twinkling against bright snow as they drove Lanesboro's main street on the way to church. That night her sweet soprano blended with the rest of the choir at Bethlehem Baptist as they belted out traditional Carols.

Made from white clapboard, Bethlehem Baptist's only distinct features were the steeple, which peaked above the small town's hilled tree tops. Eight stained glass windows, four to a side, made the sanctuary glow. All of them had been salvaged when the original church burnt to the ground in 1937. The fire also put an end to milling in the community. The only other disaster known to Lanesboro residents happened when the Root River overflowed its bank.

Every Christmas red and white poinsettias decorated the church dais. The sanctuary, bathed with flickering candles, welcomed the usual cast of parishioners. Becky smiled at her dad as he came forward to assist with the offering. Standing with his hands clasped at his waist, he waited for the brass offering bowl to pass across the twenty rows of the church. Reverend Abel invited everyone to stay for coffee, punch, and the scrumptious Christmas cookies Martha's circle had prepared before leading the congregation in the hymn they always sang at the close of each service:

> Blest be the tie that binds
> Our hearts in Christian love;
> The fellowship of kindred minds
> Is like to that above.
>
> Before our Father's throne
> We pour our ardent prayers;
> Our fears, our hopes, our aims are one
> Our comforts and our cares.
>
> We share each other's woes,
> Our mutual burdens bear;
> And often for each other flows
> The sympathizing tear.
>
> Blest be the tie that binds
> Our hearts in Christian love.

Within weeks Bethlehem Baptist's congregation was called upon to show its Christian love for the Hanson family in their time of deep sorrow. Years later, when the curtain that had covered the truth of Becky's passing was finally drawn, this tight-knit community's tears flowed like the Root River in spring.

He cased her place. Two names, B. Hanson and K. Hanson, were listed on the mail box. Couple of times hanging around outside the clinic, He spotted her on the walk home.

Must get through her shift around 3:30

Torgerson hung back a block or so—watched her hair swing across her shoulders.

"Let's bump up the lights," Carol Burnett said to her audience on the first Friday of the new year. "Who's got a question?" Burnett asked shading her eyes to search across the live audience.

"I do," a young woman responded. "Have you ever taken acting lessons?"

"Yes, I have," Burnett smiled wide.

"Do you think it did any good?" the woman added without thinking.

Bonnie and Becky laughed in-sync with the audience's reaction to Burnett's dead-pan. Other than Burnett, Tim Conway was their favorite regular on the show especially when he made Harvey Korman stifle a laugh. The wall phone in the kitchen rang while Burnett sang her famous closing song,

> I'm so glad we had this time together
> Just to have a laugh or sing a song
> Seems we just get started and before
> you know it comes the time we have to say,
> so long.

Squashing her cigarette butt in the ashtray on the counter, Becky picked up by the fourth ring. "Hello," she said expecting to hear her mother's chipper voice on the other end.

"I'm coming to rob you next week," a male voice stated. "Will you be home?"

"Not if you're going to rob us!" Becky replied, hanging up the phone.

"What was that?" Bonnie asked.

"I dunno, kinda dumb. Some guy says he's planning to rob us and wanted to know if we'll be here," Becky laughed.

"Probably a bunch of teenage boys making prank calls," Bonnie said, as she turned off the TV set. "I'm going to shower before I hit the hay. Do you need to use the bathroom first?"

The door was open—no need for the screwdriver to jimmy the lock. He just walked in. Her eyes lit with fear when she saw him standing in the kitchen just off the front room. She ran for the front door, turned the handle but it was locked. He grabbed the back of her hair, which came off in his hand: a hair piece. Her real hair hung straight just below her ear.

She twirled; escaped but Torgerson caught her at the beginning of the hallway, banged her up against the wall. Anger spread inside him like North Dakota prairie fire. They struggled into the bedroom where she grabbed the dresser. He had his hands clear around her tiny neck. She passed out. He threw her on the bed and ran to fetch the brick he had left in the front room. He smashed the side of her face. Thunk.

Yup. She's dead.

He fished out a can of lighter fluid along with a book of matches from his front shirt pocket.

Bonnie got home from work at her usual time, around quarter after five. Turning the door knob of their third floor apartment, she was surprised to find it locked. Becky must have locked it by mistake, she thought, as she rang the doorbell. No one answered. Smoke was curling out from under the door. Bonnie ran down three flights of stairs to alert the building caretaker who called 911. The fire department was dispatched at 5:20 p.m., and the police followed minutes later.

Grabbing her pass key the caretaker rushed back upstairs with Bonnie. As soon as she got the door open thick smoke pushed into the hall. In an automatic response, the caretaker closed the door. Eyes clenched tight they backed down the hall coughing, and then the caretaker clutched Bonnie by the arm directing her down the stairs.

The fire fighters found Becky Hanson lying face up on her bed. Part of her blouse was burned away, exposing a charred white brassiere. Her right ear, burnt black, resembled a shriveled mushroom. Deep burns ran down her neck and across her right shoulder. Beet-red gullies cut deep into mounds of charred tissue where a soft cheek should have been. Her lips, burned plum, exposed back molars—the coffin would be closed.

Police officer Mueller was the first cop to arrive. R&I Officer Miller showed up to take pictures and whatever else needed to be done. Chief Stai and Corner Wellner were right on their heels. When the coroner rolled the dead girl over, he saw a Mayo Clinic General Service uniform encased in a plastic bag. Blue letters spelled out 'Dison Cleaners' across the white protective inner sleeve.

In his canvass of the apartment building, Officer Mueller found no one home on the top floor. So he moved to the second floor unit directly beneath the Hanson girls' apartment. A gray-haired woman, who appeared to be in her seventies, opened her door a crack after Miller announced he was a police officer and flashed his badge.

"Oh, officer, I'm glad to see you," Myrtle Brown told Mueller. "Someone rang my buzzer right after my Perry Mason episode. I watch that every day, you know."

"Yes, ma'am," Miller politely replied, his pen poised to take notes.

"Well, by the time I got to my door someone was jiggling the knob trying to push it open. Land-a-Goshen, I was scared. Before I could call this in the sirens started wailing and all…" It took a few minutes before Mueller learned a thumping noise coming from the upstairs unit had disturbed Myrtle Brown's enjoyment of her favorite TV show.

"The noise started above me," Myrtle said pursing her thin lips. "Then it moved into the back bedroom."

Officer Mueller went back upstairs to see if he could spot signs of struggle. Because the dead girl had a slight gash on her right temple and several bruises on the left side of her neck, Mueller looked around for an object that might cause the injury. Peering under the bed, he used his pen to fish out a red patent-leather handbag, which was empty.

When he opened the closet, Mueller saw a red brick on the floor. He bagged both the purse and the brick.

Torgerson took a swig of his third Budweiser as he watched the local newscast. Just as they were wrapping-up the six o'clock broadcast, the camera panned to the outside of her apartment building, which made him sit-up and pay attention.

KTTC's seasoned anchorman voiced over, "We bring you BREAKING NEWS: Just minutes ago the body of a young woman was taken from an apartment building on Fourth Street."

The camera turned to a young reporter bundled against the cold wind. "Although a definitive cause of death has not been determined in this case," the cub reporter's said, "investigators' lead theory is that the young woman's death was caused by careless smoking. Careless smoking is the second leading cause of fire death; more than 4000 people die each year. Back to you, Dick," the street reporter announced as the picture cut back to the studio news desk.

"The name of the victim is being withheld until family notification," Rochester's most reliable news anchor reported. "We will bring you more details as they unfold."

> Wow, how the hell did they come up with that? There wasn't even an ashtray on the bed stand.

An autopsy was ordered. Finding traces of soot in Rebecca Hanson's lungs and windpipe, Dr. Wellner, who conducted the postmortem, told Chief Macken that Rebecca Hanson died as a result of smoke asphyxiation.

"The wound's superficial and, therefore, not indicative of foul play," the doctor said, responding to Chief Macken's question about the gash on her forehead.

"So we can let this go, huh, doc?" Macken grunted, his face showing relief—accidents are easier to explain away, people don't want worry something like this could happen to them. Ending the investigation was a good thing for the community, for the squad.

Four days later the coroner filed Rebecca Hanson's death certificate. It read:

line 20 Part I - Death was caused by:
A: immediate cause
Asphyxia
B: due to or as a consequence of
Mattress fire

line 22 accident, suicide, homicide or undetermined
Accident

The Hanson's could not believe it. They had questions. Questions about the extent of their daughter's injuries, questions about the $37 dollars missing from Becky's purse, and questions about the brick found in the closet.

"Becky *NEVER* smoked in bed," her mother told Officer Mueller with as much heat as her voice had ever carried. "She is—was—not a careless girl. Please," she implored, "continue the investigation."

"In our opinion, continuing the investigation would do nothing more than arouse nervous conversation and unwarranted suspicions," Mueller replied. "Hire a private investigator if you want, but as far as the department is concerned, this case is closed." Mueller was a good cop, but he knew better than to buck his boss.

Three years later Detective Mueller would be assigned to gather background information on David Torgerson for FBI Agent Mahler.

23

Anne Hogan February 16, 1970

I only wanted to rob her.

Anne Hogan was standing on a street corner waiting for the light to change. Winter started early that year, way back in the middle of November. Thirty-one inches of snow fell before Christmas. Then January's cold north winds froze the snow mounds creating sharp ice ruts on the sides of the city streets. Two days after Valentine's Day the temperature felt closer to zero than the day's actual reading of twenty-two degrees because of the wind chill factor. David Torgerson got into the driver's seat of the Chevy van and cranked the motor. He tried again and again until only the click of the key could be heard. He grabbed the newspaper from the front seat, tucked it inside his coat under his armpit, and set out on foot.

Anne reached the corner across from her apartment building. She pushed the walk button and stomped her boots, impatient to cross the street and get inside. Clouded puffs of air skated out of her nostrils. He walked down behind the houses for a couple of minutes and then cut over to the city street. His glasses steamed up and because of that he slipped and sild over the icy bumps sprinkling the sidewalk. He used his hands like an airplane to keep his balance.

Having grown up in Iowa, Anne had had her belly full of Midwest winters. Someday I'll live where it doesn't snow, she thought. A nurse can take her skills anywhere. I just need to get this first year of experience under my belt. I know Mayo Clinic will look good on my resume.

"Hey, you live around here?" a voice interrupted her daydream. "I'm looking for an apartment," the man said, removing the folded newspaper from under his arm and extending it forward as proof.

"Yeah, over there, but we don't have any vacancies," she replied motioning across the street. "Nobody wants to move much in the winter." As the stop light changed he walked by her side, across the road and right up the sidewalk to her apartment building's entrance.

"Mind if I come into the hallway to warm-up, read the paper?" Opening the front door of the apartment building for her like a gentleman, he stood still while she got her mail, and then just followed her up the stairs.

Anne opened her apartment door, stepped inside, and flipped on the light. He slipped behind her back, moved to the sofa and sat down. By the time she saw him he had opened the paper and started scanning the want ads.

"What the . . . ?" Anne murmured to herself. Shaking her head to clear her vision, Anne stared at the stranger who had come in from the cold. He felt her eyes on him and her hesitation

Anne hung her coat, returned, opened her mail, and then went into the kitchen to pour herself a glass of water.

This sure feels funny, weird even, she thought to herself. Maybe I should say something.

He heard her shoes click off a half dozen steps down the hallway. A bi-fold door scraped open and a hanger clacked against the closet rod.

After leaving the closet, Anne turned left and walked down the hall and entered her bedroom. She rounded the bed and slid into the bathroom. The door shut without making any noise but the door lock always clicked. Anne knocked on the far door before turning the handle to open it a crack. In a low voice she called out, "Sue, you here?"

"Yeah, come on in."

After passing through an apartment identical to her own, Anne found Sue cooking pasta in her kitchen. Except for their adjoining bath, their apartments were entirely separate. Since each unit had an exterior hallway entrance; no one would suspect that their apartments were linked in this fashion. It worked out well for them. The girls locked the opposite side bathroom door only when it was in use.

"What's up? You want some coffee or somethin'?" Sue asked Anne.

"No, thanks. I'm kinda confused. There's this strange guy in my apartment and…"

"A strange guy is in your apartment?"

Anne drummed her fingers on Sue's countertop. "Yeah, he followed me in when I came home from work. Said he was cold, needed a place to read the paper 'cuz he's looking for an apartment."

"Did you ask him in?"

"No, he just sorta ended up there. I didn't exactly know what to say. Then he sat down and started reading the paper. Been there awhile now. What should I do?"

"Is he cute? Sue asked.

Anne gave her the fish eye.

"Guess not. Golly Gee, I dunno. Maybe he's gone by now. Why don't you go see."

After finding the stranger hadn't moved a muscle, Anne pulled a chair out (one that gave her a clear view of the front room) from the kitchen table and took a checkbook out of her purse. While she paid her bills she looked up every once in a while to glance in his direction. He kept his eyes on the newspaper. For a while neither of them spoke. He broke the silence.

"Warm in here. Got some music?"

"Yeah, good idea," Anne said. "I like to listen during chores, almost makes it fun." Kneeling on the worn living room carpet she pulled albums from the bookcase. "Beatles or Crosby, Stills and Nash?"

"Nice pad."

"Gee Thanks. Okay, then. Beatles first, The White Album."

As the strains of 'Martha Dear' filled the apartment, the discomfort ebbed. As soon as she finished paying her bills, Ann carried her junk mail and torn envelopes to the kitchen trash bin located under the sink. The dirty dishes, piled on the counter from last night's dinner and this morning's breakfast, called out to her. Guess I'll do these up, she thought while sighing out loud. Maybe if I rattle the pots and pans enough he'll get the hint and just leave.

> I hope her legs twitch. Maybe she'll kick
> a little bit like the first one, the little girl;
> her heels slapped against my thighs.

Anne put on the next album and then went back into her bedroom to change out of her work clothes, which was when her gut told her something's was really not right, so she headed back to Sue's to talk it over some more.

"I'm getting kinda creeped out. He's been sitting there a long time now."

"Okay, let's call the guys across the street," Sue suggested grabbing the phone. "See what they say."

Anne hesitated, it's the seventies after all and she thought a woman should stand on her own two feet. She didn't want anyone thinking: there goes another dependent, helpless female who can't take care of herself.

Sue cocked her head and raised an eyebrow.

"Alright, sure, yeah. Guess I could use some advice."

Ron Marcou, also known as Bear, answered on the first ring. Big, strong and shaggy haired, 'Bear' played defensive end in high school and college. When opponents mistook his stocky legs and lumbering gait as a sign of weakness, he made them pay. He could sprint down the field near the pace of his roommate John Riester, a track and field athlete. Bear's toothy grin and mellow manner drew girls to him off the field.

"Bear," he said in a deep baritone.

"Hi-ah, it's Sue. I'm calling for Anne, she's here and well…" Sue played with the long, spiral phone cord as she switched her weight from one foot to the other.

"Somethin' wrong?"

"There's a guy in her apartment," Sue said in a rush. "And she don't know him."

"Huh. Let me talk at her."

"How'd this fella end up at your place?" Bear asked Anne.

"He just sorta walked in, you know. Walked me across the street. Said he needed a warm place to read the paper because he's trying to find an apartment. I dunno, I feel kinda dumb," Anne said, embarrassment lifting up her neck like steam curling out of a manhole cover in the dead of winter.

"What's he look like?" Bear asked.

"Oh, mousey, I guess. Non-descript. Tall, thin."

"And he just sits there reading? Hasn't tried to ask you out or nothin'?"

"Uh, huh."

"Sounds harmless, no big deal," Bear reassured her. "Just go home and shoo him out. If he refuses, I'll show him the door." Bear's roommates laughed when he told them how this fellow ended up sitting on Anne's couch.

"We gotta try that one out next time we wanna pick a girl up," John snorted.

Half-an-hour later Anne's scream made Sue's skin crawl. She knew there was trouble next door, big trouble. Sue ran across the street, coatless and in slippers, to get the guys. They barreled out of their apartment, crossed the icy street, took the stairs two at a time, pummeled through Emily's open hall door, dodged her furniture and ended up catapulting into Anne's bedroom from the girls' shared bath. Three minutes had ticked off the clock since Sue first heard Anne scream.

Bear burst through the door first and saw Torgerson on top of Anne pushing down hard on the pillow covering her face. He put an arm-lock around Torgerson's neck, pulled back and up, before tossing him aside. Torgerson flew through the air like a football. After he got to his feet, he wobbled and then gained a foothold. And then John tackled him full force. Sue's shrill wail turned to sobs as soon as she saw Anne's black and blue mottled face. She was unconscious.

"John, get Sue the hell outta here," Bear growled. "Call 911."

Part Three

In human affairs there must be a clear distinction between the penalties for small and great crimes. Retribution for wrong doing must be swiftly applied if greater problems are to be prevented.

I Ching

The world is a dangerous place to live, not because of the people who are evil, but because of the people who don't do anything about it.

Albert Einstein

24

George Head, who hailed from Rochester, New York, founded a Minnesota village in 1854 on the South Fork of the Zumbro River by driving a white hand-painted stake into the ground. Black letters spelled out 'Rochester.' The name stuck. Head's original land claim became the heart of the city's business district. In 1958 Rochester's modern county courthouse, (a cold, sleek two-story building) was built for efficiency, not grandeur like its Victorian predecessor. Its work counters opened directly into the hall to better serve the citizens of Olmsted County. David Torgerson's first hearing, for assaulting Anne Hogan, took place in the main courtroom on March 2, 1970.

Richard Gullickson, appointed to defend Torgerson, was a lanky six-footer who could almost be considered a home town boy having grown up in nearby Zumbrota Falls. Gullickson attended Winona State straight from high school and, after earning a degree in political science there, he headed off to law school at the University of Minnesota in the twin cities. He had come home to build a law practice. Since court appointments like this one made up thirty-percent of his revenue, Richard Gullickson was eager to showcase his skills. He wanted to do well with this case so more business would be funneled his way.

Olmsted County prosecutor Dan Mattson's graying temples, tailored suit, monogrammed shirt and buffed wingtips signified a much more seasoned litigator. He knew his way around the courthouse. Plea bargains provided a way to clear the docket and they were a quick way to put a checkmark in his win column. Mattson was proud of his ninety-eight percent conviction rate.

Mattson had replaced the county's former lead prosecutor, Kenneth Schoen, last year when Schoen became Minnesota's Commissioner of Corrections. Some say Schoen's appointment came about because of his collaboration with Dr. Tyce (Torgerson's psychiatrist) PORT (Probationed Offenders Rehabilitation and Training) Program.

Mattson saw his prosecutorial office as a stepping-stone to becoming a judge. He thought he might even replace Judge Franke. They talked about it once or twice. Franke told him how he sometimes thought about wintering in Palm Springs. How great it would be to play golf there year round. Anyway, it wouldn't be this year. Mattson could see that Judge Franke was still invested in his job and the community.

The Honorable William S. Franke, known for his acrid wit in social circles and no-nonsense attitude on the bench, presided over Torgerson's trial. A consummate jurist, he used his bench to instruct. He loved the law, the letter of it, and liked to wade right in on matters of interpretation. Sonya Williams, his clerk of court, would tell you he was also a compassionate man. When her granddaughter needed heart surgery, he told her to take all the time she needed. "Family's important," he'd said. Sonya's heart tugged whenever she thought about how he sent flowers and a stuffed teddy bear to the hospital.

On the first day of testimony the State called Anne Hogan as its first witness. Wanting to be taken seriously, she had picked out a simple blouse and plain navy skirt to wear for this court appearance. She stated her name, age (23), occupation, address and marital status (single) for the record before identifying David James Torgerson as the man who had been in her apartment on the 16th day of February, 1970.

"Miss Hogan, can you first of all, briefly tell the Court how the defendant, David Torgerson, came to be in your apartment?" Prosecutor Mattson asked.

"He met me on the street corner across the street from my house and asked if he could sit in the hallway to warm up, and then he followed me up the stairs. When I went to turn on the light he came inside so I told him to sit down.

"He wanted to read the newspaper—he was there a little over an hour. I went to my bedroom and he grabbed me. I screamed. He covered my mouth to cut off the scream and," Anne's voice breaks, trails off. "And the last thing I remembered was him choking me."

"When you woke up…" Mattson took a moment, backed up. "You passed out, didn't you?"

"Yes."

"When you woke up, who was in the room?"

"Bear—Ron Marcou—and the police, I guess. I'm not sure."

"Some police officers. Was the defendant there then, too?"

"I didn't think so, but I guess he was."

"Now, in the time he was in your…" Mattson paused for a beat. "You had left the room, had you not?"

"Yes."

"What did you leave the room for?"

"Well, I read my mail, did my dishes, changed my clothes, and was talking to the girl next door."

"Can you tell the Court why you went next door?"

"I went next door to tell her this strange fellow was in my living room and what was I to do to get rid of him."

Before Mattson yielded the floor he had Hogan describe her injuries.

"I have just a couple of questions, your Honor," Gullickson said, putting his hands on the desk top to brace himself before approaching the witness stand.

"When did you go next door to visit with this other girl?"

"I went as soon as I got home, and I went back and forth. We share a bathroom so I was just going back and forth from the bathroom."

"And he was there, in your apartment, for more than an hour?"

"Yes."

"That's it, your Honor," Gullickson said before returning to sit next to his client.

After being sworn in, the next witness, Detective Bryon Heinen, responded to a few perfunctory questions about himself before the prosecutor led him through the preliminary data concerning his first meeting with the defendant.

"All right, officer, please tell the Court what you did as far as your investigation is concerned, particularly with reference to any statements that were taken from him,"

Mattson asked motioning toward Torgerson. "Tell us just exactly what occurred in chronological order."

"I was notified at 7:48 p.m. on the 16th of February that an assault had taken place—"

"Your Honor, hearsay evidence," Gullickson interjected.

"How were you notified, through what?" Mattson asked, ignoring Gullickson objection.

Officer Heinen replied, "I learned of the assault from the police dispatcher."

Turning to address the court, Mattson countered Gullickson's motion, "This is an exception, Your Honor. Reliable hearsay evidence is admissible in a preliminary hearing, as I understand it."

Judge Franke concurred and overruled the defense's objection.

Officer Heinen then testified he met the assault victim, Anne Hogan, at the police station and while taking her statement noticed she had bruises on her neck that she attributed to her attacker. "I took photographs of her neck and then sent her home with a neighbor who had accompanied her to the police station."

Mattson took a sip of water as he scanned the notes he'd made on a yellow legal pad. He had to get this next part right, ask precise questions. If the defense could show anything improper about Heinen's Miranda Warning of Torgerson, the case would be dismissed.

"All right, officer, now about the Miranda Warning, could you tell the Court, please, exactly what you informed the defendant concerning his constitutional rights."

"I informed David James Torgerson of his right to remain silent; that anything he told me would be used against him in a Court of Law. I informed him of his right to an attorney, to have an attorney present before any questioning and, if he could not afford to retain an attorney, one could be appointed before any questioning. Then I asked Mr. Torgerson if he fully understood the constitutional rights just given to him. He said he did and was willing to talk about the incident."

"Now, this was done before any statements concerning this crime were elicited from him?" Mattson prompted the officer.

"That is correct. This was before any questioning was made."

"Who else was present during that time?" Mattson's asked the officer.

"I'm sorry, I can't recall which officer. There was an officer on guard, but I don't recall the officer's name at this point."

"Torgerson's statement was reduced to writing, is that correct?"

"Yes sir."

"And was the statement that you got from him… Was it taken by the secretary or something? Was that transcribed?"

"His statement was tape recorded. Then on the following day, February 17, the Miranda Warning was given to him in writing," Heinen said, looking the prosecutor straight on. "I also gave him a typed copy of his statement, his accounting of the events, to check over. And then I had him sign the Miranda warning."

"All right," Mattson flashed a confident smile. "Were any promises of leniency or reward or any inducements of any kind given to him in order to induce him to give you a statement?"

"No promises, whatsoever, were given him," Heinen responded, his face settled, devoid of emotion.

"Any threats made toward him?"

"No threats of any kind."

"Please tell the Court then what he told you? In other words, what went into the tape recording, what was said concerning what he did to Anne Hogan on the 16th day of February."

Gullickson stood to object. He asserted the defendant did not fully understand the nature or the ramifications of the Miranda Warning because of his mental condition.

"There is no evidence to support that." Mattson replied in a clipped voice.

Judge Franke intervened wagging his pen back-and-forth in the air as if he were separating the two tables. "Now tell the court, if you will counselor, does your objection rise out of your concern for Mr. Torgerson's lack of understanding at the time the warning was given or are you objecting as a result of a subsequent conversation you have had with the defendant?"

"At the time it was given," Gullickson said with conviction.

Mattson jumped to his feet. "Your Honor defense counsel is asking the court to draw a conclusion. There is no evidence to base that upon. He (Torgerson) says he did. This is all we have got to go by."

"That is what I want to know. I want to know whether he was saying that at the time or whether he is saying that now," Judge Franke scolded.

"I'm making this for the record, your Honor, because obviously..." Gullickson looked down, shuffled papers. "If the Court binds the defendant over to District Court, I intend to, ask for a psychiatric evaluation."

"Well, there is no evidence before the Court right now that the defendant wasn't perfectly normal at the time this occurred, except that the actual incidents certainly are not the usual actions of an average person," Judge Franke declared.

"Whenever an individual does not do what we think of as standard behavior, it doesn't mean he needs psychiatric help. The courts are, of course, very lenient now," Judge Franke said, looking over his wire-rim glasses at the near empty courtroom. "Every one that commits a crime—there is something the matter with them or they wouldn't have committed the crime—ergo they are not guilty of anything.

"How is the Court going to prove that? How are we going to prove what this man understood about the matter? He kept telling the police he understood the whole thing the whole time. Now we run into the situation where he says he didn't understand it.

"Well, what did he say then? I mean, he is not a child. He is of age I take it. I guess he is over 18. The prosecutor is saying is he indicated he understood it all. And now he says he didn't understand it," the judge said, shaking his head like a dog clearing water out of its ears after taking a dip in the lake.

"The only thing the Court can go on is the record or what evidence is before the Court as to what was actually said and what he said. There is no way to honor the protection of the people if anyone can say, 'I didn't understand it, your Honor.' I mean, understanding the Miranda Warning is the only thing he has to understand. I take it you have talked to this man as your client?"

"Yes," Gullickson replied.

"Does he seem to understand what you say?" the judge asked staring down at the defense table.

"I believe to some extent, Your Honor, there is a certain amount of confusion on the various ramifications in the legal proceedings and the involvement…"

Exasperated, Judge Franke interrupted, "We don't expect him to understand the Miranda Warning, because I don't think anybody in this room understands it! It would be hardly possible for him to understand it, to have that high a standard. In fact, there are a great many courts who don't understand it, including this one, as far as the legal side of it goes. But the substance of it—that this would be used against him. Do you think he understood that?"

"I would suspect not, Your Honor, in light of his past history," Gullickson responded.

Judge Franke shifted in his chair. "Did he know he was in the police department?"

"I suspect he did."

"Did he know that he was being investigated for a possible charge of a criminal action?

"I suspect he understood there was some investigation under way by reason of being at a police station, but from that point on…"

"From that point on he immediately became blank, is that right?" Judge Franke said, his voice going up an octave.

Gullickson adjusted his tie before replying. "I think as to understanding the full nature of the situation and the fact that he could have had counsel with him and that he could have remained silent, I think these things are still somewhat confusing to him. Obviously, I am not a psychiatrist. I brought it up as a matter for the record. I realize the Court's position… that unless we have some medical evidence the Court would have to take the foundation established by the officer and make a proper ruling."

"Well, your objection was that he did not understand it. There is no evidence before the Court that he did not understand it, and, of course, one begs the question of the other, whether he understood it or not. At least he indicated he did and, of course, that's all the police department had to go on." The judge stopped to draw a breath. "If he had said, 'No, I don't understand it' or 'I want an attorney' or 'No' to any of these questions, it would have been dropped, but, you see, what people do is come in and say yes to everything, and then when they get to court they say I didn't understand any part of it… And, of course, the police take every precaution to try to make the defendant understand what his rights are.

"They try to give the Miranda Warning as it is stated; they also go further than that, and they try to find out whether the defendant understands it or not. They even go that far. But the question here is whether the defendant must take responsibility when asked a question. He has to take the responsibility of answering, and in this case he answered, 'Yes.'

"Now, I don't know the defendant, what he does or what his background is, but at least he is not in an institution, he is walking around in the public, and allowed to walk up and down our streets. He has got to take some responsibility," Judge Franke declared, witha hint of disgust in his timbre. "And one would be answering questions; simple questions that are asked. So as far as this court is concerned there is no evidence that the defendant did not understand the Miranda Warning or what he was there for."

Waving his hand in the prosecutor's direction, Judge Franke indicated Mattson was free to continue his direct examination of Officer Heinen. Heinen told the Court he informed Torgerson of Anne Hogan's complaint against him of assault. "Then I asked him to tell me, in his own words, what had happened."

"Do you have that statement with you today?" Prosecutor Mattson asked.

Heinen nodded as he pulled out his report and then he read Torgerson's signed statement into the record:

> I saw this girl. And I noticed she was carrying a purse but I didn't get the chance to take it so I made up a story about hunting for an apartment and asked to warm up in her hallway. I just followed her into the apartment. I was only there to steal her purse. It wasn't in the living room so I had to follow her into her bedroom to get it. I must have bumped her or somethin' because she screamed. I had to quiet her. I grabbed her by the throat and choked her for a short time. She went limp and dropped to the floor. It was pure panic. I didn't plan it or nothin'.

In his cross examination, Gullickson asked Heinen three questions: what was the length of time Torgerson stayed in Ann Hogan's apartment, did they play records, and did he know if she offered Torgerson coffee. After the court excused Officer Heinen, Mattson rested the state's case.

"Does the defense plan to present any evidence?" the Judge asked Gullickson.

"None, your Honor, but I do request a psychiatric evaluation of my client to determine if he is capable of understanding the charges against him."

Judge Franke granted the motion and then said, "If there is no objection the court will appoint Dr. Frederick Tyce to conduct the evaluation."

Neither table responded so the judge moved forward. "Okay then, the record will show that the defendant does not wish to present any evidence at this hearing. It is the judgment of the Court that the defendant may be guilty of a crime; that there is probable cause to believe that the defendant committed the crime as charged, and that the defendant will be bound over to District Court in one month's time. The bond ($5000.00) will remain the same."

Judge Franke banged his gavel.

The lawyers gathered up their briefs and shoved them into their standard issue black bags.

25

Two weeks before the continuation of Torgerson's hearing Mattson called defense attorney, Richard Gullickson.

"Let's make a deal, Dick," Mattson proposed. "Move this thing along."

"What's the offer?"

"We'll drop the assault. Simple robbery. He pleads guilty."

"How much time?"

"Judge Franke is a good guy. Most likely he'll follow the sentencing guidelines—give him the minimum, one-to-three."

"I'll talk to my client and get back to you."

"Tell him it's a no brainer," Mattson advised. "Show him Dr. Tyce's letter. He says your guy's competent, knew what was going on when he confessed to the police. You make the motion, the state won't object. If he keeps his nose clean he'll be out in fourteen months. It's a good deal. He should take it."

On April 17, 1970, Gullickson drew his client to his feet as the clerk of court announced, "Hear Ye, Hear Ye, all rise in the matter before this court on behalf of the State of Minnesota versus David J. Torgerson. The Honorable Donald T. Franke presiding."

After the judge was seated Gullickson stood to say, "Your Honor, I have conferred with my learned counsel and we have agreed to amend the second degree charge of assault to one of simple robbery."

"The State concurs?" Franke asked looking at the prosecutor.

"We do, Your Honor," Mattson responded.

"Alright then, the defense will please read the formal charge into the record."

Gullickson cleared his throat and read the following charge out loud, "David J. Torgerson did willfully, wrongfully, intentionally and feloniously attempt to commit simple robbery from one Anne Hogan."

After establishing that all of Torgerson's constitutional rights had been met, Judge Franke asked for the defendant's plea. Gullickson touched Torgerson's arm directing him to his feet.

"I feel I should plead guilty," Torgerson said, hanging his head.

"What do you mean? Has anyone coerced you into pleading guilty to this charge?" the judge inquired.

"No sir."

"If the court is to proceed, you need to plead guilty without reservation. Am I making myself clear?"

"Yes sir. I am sorry. I plead guilty."

Satisfied with Torgerson's answer, Judge Franke rocked back in his chair and listened while the prosecution outlined the basic facts of the case. After Mattson finished the statement of fact, the judge swiveled his chair. Lifting his chin he motioned defense counsel to rise. "Mr. Gullickson, is there anything else you would like to state for the record at this point?"

"Yes, Judge. With regard to the crime in question, Your Honor, the defendant was financially destitute," Gullickson eyeballed his client hoping he looked appropriately despondent.

Torgerson's face was blank.

"He has a wife and a young daughter, born last December. He was out of a job and had been looking for work and I suspect out of desperation thought perhaps he could pick up a few dollars by way of his attempted robbery."

The judge dipped his head up then down, in quick succession to acknowledge he understood defense counsel's reasoning.

"He had spent over an hour in the young lady's apartment and it's his contention that when he walked into her bedroom she screamed. And then he became frantic or excited—attempted to stop the screaming—and I think over reacted to the situation." Gullickson sighed.

Judge Franke nodded to show he was listening.

Gullickson took a sip of water, cleared his throat and continued, "He had previously worked at Waters Company. He quit in December of 1969 in anticipation of going into the service. Even though he had passed his physical examination, Your Honor, at first he was rejected because of his family status, having a wife and one child as dependents.

"Still he persisted and the recruiter showed renewed interest. Ultimately they rejected him on the basis of his confinement to the Rochester State Hospital, which the court was advised of in Dr. Tyce's letter, dated April 6.

"The court should note Dr. Tyce found the defendant to have a normal range of intellectual functioning and there is no area of particular impairment. It was just an overreaction to a rather desperate frantic situation. He has had time to think about it—being confined in the county jail since mid-February. We feel that a probationary period would be a big help to this man rather than prison."

"Thank you counsel," Judge Franke said. "Now, I want to hear from the defendant. Bailiff. will you please swear Mr. Torgerson in?"

After establishing his age and current address, the Judge asked Torgerson about his work history. Torgerson stated he worked for five months in Texas as a metal mold fabricator and had most recently worked for Waters Company of Rochester but quit that job in anticipation of entering the army. Revealing he had also worked at the Ability Building Center when he was as a resident at Rochester State Mental Hospital, Torgerson testified, "Anyway, I quit that (ABC employment) when I got discharged and I had been there for, I don't know, for about eight years. I wanted to see the country, you know."

"I see. Let's turn then to your personal history. Please verify for the record your date and place of birth."

"July 13, 1943. Austin, Minnesota."

When asked about his parents, Torgerson said he did not know where they currently lived. For a moment, Judge Franke felt confused until he realized the motherly figure present in the court was not Torgerson's own mother, but rather his mother-in-law, Darlene Knutson. Her presence coupled with Torgerson's baby-face and milquetoast demeanor softened the judge. After brief questions about Torgerson's marriage and the birth of his child, Sylvia, Judge Franke sought out more information concerning Torgerson's formative years.

Torgerson reported he attended school until the eleventh grade and then supplied a vague, "I am sorry but I can't remember that," when asked how long ago he left high school.

"It was probably eight or nine years ago, would that be right?" Judge Franke prompted.

"Oh, it would probably be in 1959 because I had to go to the hospital—I went to the hospital in 1959," Torgerson replied, opening up the issue of his confinement at Rochester State Mental Hospital for discussion.

"You went to the Rochester State Hospital?" Judge Franke repeated.

"Yes. Probably," Torgerson equivocated.

"Rochester State Hospital, that's the hospital that treated you for your psychiatric or mental problems, right?"

"Yes sir."

"Do you recall whether you were committed by a probate court or did you go voluntarily, on what is called a self-committed basis?"

"Court-committed."

"Do you recall anything particular that you did—the reason for the commitment? Any unusual behavior that started this problem?" Judge Franke asked.

"For the reason I went to the hospital?" Torgerson stalled for a moment before he said, "I really can't define it."

"Problems with your parents?" Judge Franke asked.

"I think that was one, pretty much. I overcome that a longtime ago but I am sure it had an awful lot to do with it. Because they sort of rejected…I had the feeling they rejected me. It seems like they always…"

"Blamed you for what went wrong, that kind of thing?" the judge filled in.

"My brothers and sisters—they always got more than I did," Torgerson said, holding complaint from his voice.

Gullickson had told him not to bellyache, 'Just keep your tone level and your answers short,' he'd advised.

"Everybody else was better and you felt you were the black sheep?" Judge Franke continued.

"That's it," Torgerson said, happy to escape having to talk about the real reason for his hospital commitment.

"You still feel that way?" Judge Franke asked, cocking an ear.

"No, of course not," Torgerson said, fast as he could.

"You still had problems and you recognized that?" the judge reiterated.

"Yes, sir," Torgerson said.

"But you don't think these problems are somebody else's fault do you, or do you?" Judge Franke asked for the last time.

"No. I am more mature on it now," Torgerson said.

After Prosecutor Mattson stated the facts of the case for the record, Judge Franke turned back to the defendant. "Mr. Torgerson, you just heard Mr. Mattson summarize the essential facts presented in the preliminary hearing. What the Hogan girl testified to on the witness stand down in Municipal Court didn't you?"

"Yes, Your Honor."

"Do you agree with the version that was summarized by Mr. Mattson?"

"Essentially, but he did mention where—and maybe it is just the way I took it—he said I choked her and then intended to rob her. I didn't like that part. I only went there with the intention to rob her, sir. Not the other."

"In her bedroom?"

"Yes. But it wasn't an afterthought. It was a before thought, the robbery, Your Honor."

"You were thinking of trying to get some money?"

"Yes, sir," Torgerson said. "I had no intention of hurting her."

"You thought there might be some money in the bedroom?" Judge Franke's asked with a cocked eyebrow.

"Well, I couldn't find her purse in the kitchen and I couldn't find it in the living room," Torgerson explained.

"Did you look for it? So you went around and checked the place while she was in the bedroom. You couldn't find it so you figured it was in the bedroom?"

"I did look around, yes, and then I thought I would look in the bedroom. If it wasn't there I was going to leave," Torgerson replied

"Can you tell me about how you came to be in her apartment in the first place? You asked her something about coming to get warm and then asked her if she had a newspaper. Is that right?

"Right."

"And you went up to her apartment with her to look for a newspaper? And you went into the living room of her apartment?"

"Right."

"And did she find a newspaper?"

"I had the newspaper with me."

"Oh, you had one with you? You just wanted to..." Judge Franke paused to consider whether this information indicated malice aforethought. "What did you tell her, originally, that you wanted to go in her apartment for?"

"That I wanted to warm up."

"So you had your newspaper and you were going to use her telephone or something?"

"Yes, sir," Torgerson said as polite as an altar boy.

"Then when you stayed there… Why is it that you stayed so long?"

"It doesn't seem like it was that long," Torgerson said.

"I notice that's what you told Dr. Tyce—that you were quite surprised you were there that long? Of course, that's her estimate and she could be wrong, too," Judge Franke reflected out loud.

Torgerson quickly responded, "True."

"But you think you might have been there over an hour?"

"Probably. Because she played some records. If I remember right, each record I have always lasted at least 15 minutes."

"She played three or four records?" Franke took his glasses off, twirled them by one stem thinking. "Did you ask her to do that or did she just turn on the record player on her own?

"I asked her because I was quite nervous myself. I was actually shaking when I went in there," Torgerson said, his voice quaking. "I was more scared than she was."

"You felt that you really ought not to be there?"

"Yes sir. And I was just going to—at the last minute I wasn't going to go. She was in her bedroom," Torgerson paused, looked down and then shaking his head from side-to-side as if remembering a bad dream. "I couldn't just walk into her bedroom because she was in there and the idea of me being in there…"

"Upset her because she didn't expect you to come in there?" Judge Franke prompted.

"If her purse wasn't in there… Why I was just going to leave—so I went in there to see if it was there," Torgerson explained again.

"And in a moment of panic—you did grab her somewhere around the neck like she said, you do remember that?"

Torgerson's body tightened. He looked at his lawyer. Gullickson leaned over, whispered in his client's ear, "Keep it simple, just like we practiced—yes, sir, no sir. It's almost over."

"You do remember taking her around the neck?" Judge Franke reiterated.

"Yes sir."

"With your hands? And then she passed out."

"Yes sir. That was...I intended to, you know, until she quieted down."

"You were holding her to keep her from screaming?"

"I was going to put a sleep hold on her."

"You were going to do what?" Judge Franke's voice moved up the scale one note.

"I was—I know how to put the sleeper hold on. I was going to do that to her."

"Is that pressing a nerve to make somebody pass out?" Judge Franke asked.

"Yes. It's right here," Torgerson said, motioning toward his neck.

"In the cords of the neck, roughly?"

"Yes sir. Sort of right in here," Torgerson said, touching a spot just under his right ear. "She kept screaming, you know, and instead of pressing there I pressed on her throat."

"You felt her go limp? What did you do then?"

"Then I left her there."

Concerned about a sexual motivation for Torgerson's behavior, Judge Franke asked, "You didn't lay her on the bed or anything?"

"No sir."

"You let her go to the floor. Is that right?"

"But she didn't drop," Torgerson hurried to explain. "I was holding her."

"As you felt her relax you just laid her down?"

"Yes, that's it."

"Did you go look for the purse at that point?"

"No, I wanted to get out of there. I was just on my way out when they came busting through the door."

"Did they grab you then or did you get away?"

"I was behind the bedroom door there and they opened that. I think they asked me why I was there or something."

"Did you leave the apartment, or did they just keep you there while they called the police, and then the police picked you up at the apartment?"

"No sir. This one big guy, I wasn't going to play around with him. He was that wide," Torgerson said, throwing his arms far apart.

"One of those large policemen?" Judge Franke asked, confusion clouding his face.

"He wasn't a policeman," Torgerson replied helpfully.

"He is talking about the boy," Gullickson interrupted to explain.

"Oh, I see, this is the boy from the apartment, the one who was keeping you there until the police arrived. Oh, Okay. I see," the judge said.

"Mr. Torgerson, you mentioned the sleeper-hold. Have you ever applied that to anyone else in the past?"

"Yes sir. Me and another guy were fooling around at the hospital and I used it one time."

"This is while you were a patient out at the Rochester State Hospital?"

"Yes sir."

"Is this where you learned to do it?"

"Yes. We were doing some judo stuff, you know, in the gym," Torgerson said.

"This other fellow told you how to put a sleeper hold on somebody so they would fall asleep?" Judge Franke said.

"It was discussed quite a bit," Torgerson said, his tone flat.

"And you say you were quite good at it or he was?"

"Him. He was quite good at it."

"Have you done this more than with him?" Judge Franke's curiosity was peaked. "Have you ever applied a sleeper hold on anybody else?"

"No, it was just him. We were just goofing around," Torgerson said.

"But you, you thought of it when you were in this girl's house. It came to you that this might be a way to keep her quiet?"

"Yes, sir," Torgerson replied. "But actually it doesn't. You can still talk with the sleeper hold going on, but it only takes a matter of seconds."

"I see. Okay, then," Judge Franke conceded.

Having no interest in taking this conversation further, he informed the court, "I will read the formal plea into the record: David D. Torgerson, having pled guilty to the crime of attempted simple robbery in violation of Minnesota Statutes, it is the judgment of this court that you are guilty of this crime. Before sentence is imposed, I order a pre-sentence investigation by the Department of Corrections' of the State of Minnesota. The $5,000 bond remains."

Gullickson rose and pled with the court, "The defendant is unable to raise bond, Your Honor, as he has been confined to the jail…"

"I don't propose to change the level of the bond in view of the offense," Judge Franke said over his shoulder as he left the courtroom. As soon as the judge got to his chambers, he told Sonya to contact the parole department. "Have them appoint the next guy on the list to do a background study. They know the drill."

State Parole Agent David Flotten was assigned to prepare the pre-sentence report. When Judge Franke read Flotten's thorough report three weeks later, his face turned crimson.

26

"Sonya, get Mattson's girl on the phone. Tell her I want his ass in my chamber right now!"

"Yes sir, right away," Sonya said as she flipped through her rolodex. When Rita picked up, Sonya said, "Judge Franke's having one of his Maxfield moments. He wants your guy over here, pronto."

"Percolating, huh? Okay, I'll send him by soon as he comes in," Rita said with a laugh.

A half hour later, Mattson knocked, and then entered the judge's chamber. "You called?"

"You know 'bout any a this?" Franke snapped, flopping Flotten's thick report on the desk.

"Huh, oh that. I, uhmm...my plates been kind of full. Went to Florida for Easter. Played some golf."

"This fellow Torgerson's some kind of nut case," Judge Franke said. "He's going to kill a foolish girl some God-damn day! Gees-us, what in the Sam Hill were you thinking?"

Flotten had done his foot work. His extensive report covered fifteen, single-spaced, legal size pages. He interviewed all of the principals, taped each interview, found the pertinent Mower County police files buried in the basement, and accessed Torgerson's mental health records. His report also included a statement from the victim's (Anne Hogan) friend and neighbor, Sue Liesen.

"Thanks for coming in to meet with me, Sue." Flotten smiled at the young woman, attempting to put her at ease. "Just a couple of minutes here and you can be on your way. Why don't we start with you telling me how you learned there was a guy in Anne's apartment?"

"Yeah, Okay sure. After he refused to leave her apartment, Anne, ah-h, she came on over to my place, on account of her needing advice on how to get rid of him and all, so I, uh, I phoned the boys, you know, our neighbors, and then they tackled him until the police arrived."

"When did you realize she was in trouble?"

"I heard her scream and ran cross the street to alert the boys. We found that guy, Torgerson, sitting on top of her. Her shirt was pulled up over her head and he held this pillow tight across her face," Sue replied, tightening her arms straight out in front of her demonstrating what she had witnessed.

"Bear pulled him off and John wrestled with him and stuff. I seen she was bad off. After Anne come to she was taken to St. Mary's hospital by ambulance."

Agent Flotten learned one more detail about the assault from looking over the police file: the search of Torgerson's person yielded a knife and a screwdriver.

When Flotten interviewed him, Torgerson made a thin stab at incorporating Judge Franke's courtroom suggestion that his problems stemmed from a poor relationship with his parents.

"In the case of the ten-year-old girl, I had been having trouble with my folks and she came along at the wrong time."

I just hate this shit, Flotten thought. Just once, I'd like to hear one of these guys say, I did it. I'm responsible, instead of always trying to transfer blame.

"It was a quiet spot in the woods. I was just picking berries. I didn't even know her," Torgerson continued.

Great. Now he wants me to know there was no intent, no premeditation on his part. He was just an innocent guy there picking berries.

Flotten exhaled. I'll bet he's going try to make me feel sorry for him next.

"I knew what I was doing every second of this one and was only trying to quiet her. See. We needed money for the baby. We was two months behind on rent, car payment's past due, and there was this bad check out."

Yep, right on schedule. I'm a frickin' genius.

"I was looking for a job that day and I saw this girl while I was walking around thinking about what to do. I thought I'd snatch her purse. I was pretty cold because I had been walking for a long time."

Flotten remained silent.

Torgerson shifted in his chair, leaned forward, and kept his eyes downcast. "I stopped her on the sidewalk and asked if I could warm up in her apartment building and I was just going to take her purse when we got in there. She told me her apartment was messy. I told her I'd seen messy apartments before. She told me to go into her living room and read her paper there," Torgerson gestured, scraping his chair across the tile floor.

Looking up from his legal pad, Flotten kept his face blank.

Torgerson continued, "Then we played records and talked some. I couldn't spot her purse in the living room.

When she goes into her bedroom I come in behind her—I was just going to leave."

Torgerson paused in order to give Flotten a moment to consider his good intention.

"Then I decided to look in the bedroom for her purse. I was standing behind her and I must have bumped her or something because she screamed out. I panicked, put my hands around her throat to make her quiet down. She went limp, sank to the floor," he said, meeting Flotten's gaze before adding, quick as a prairie dog, "but I made sure she was all right."

This scumbag thinks he's outsmarting me, Flotten reflected. I got news for him. I cracked wilier guys than him in my time. Keeping his eyes level Flotten made sure he did not show Torgerson one scintilla of concern.

Anger stole across Torgerson's face. "The girl's shirt was **not** pulled over her face like them boys said," he exclaimed, sitting back hard into the grey metal folding chair.

Ah, now we're getting somewhere, Flotten thought, this guy's got some kind of tit fetish. Flotten never bought any perp's bullshit story, their justifications or excuses; he put his faith in the facts. He pulled the official police report, which included a statement taken from the victim, Anne Hogan, out from his satchel. He scanned the report before focusing on the transcript officer Heinen had made of his interview with Hogan, where the victim said:

> He followed me inside and made himself comfortable. When I finally worked up enough courage to ask him to leave he seemed okay with it. I walked him to the front door and then went on back to my bedroom. I was

> ratting my hair when I saw him in the mirror. He attacked me from behind, put his hands around my neck. I couldn't breathe. I went down and he straddled my hips. He pulled my shirt up, over my head. Grabbed a pillow off my bed and smothered me.

Then Flotten located Torgerson's family history in the Rochester State Hospital file. Near the top of the stack of papers he found a charge of neglect, dated November of 1958, against Torgerson's parents, Esther and Harold, along with a court order demanding they take their son, David, to the University of Minnesota's Hospital for evaluation. Looks like I'll be taking a field trip. Get myself on over to Austin to meet up with his parents, Flotten said to himself as he continued to sort through the numerous social work interviews that had been conducted with Torgerson's parents over a period of years. Look at this: Mom blames David's problems on her long, difficult labor and his breach delivery. Told the worker he didn't talk until he turned four. Bed-wetter too, up to the age of ten.

Flotten picked up the phone to call the Torgerson household. Esther answered the phone and seemed reluctant to have him come. Flotten persisted, making an appointment for late in the afternoon. He had learned from experience it worked best to show up right away. He drove the ninety miles over to Austin that day, arriving right before dinner.

After settling the niceties, Flotten said, "Why don't we start with the reason your son, David, was committed to Rochester State Hospital." Esther looked away and Harold stared a hole straight through him. They all remained silent for what seemed like a long time.

"What have you ever done for us?" Harold said. His voice filled with accusation, "You government workers. You got your ways. Don't bother us none with no more of your stupid questions."

"How about your other children. Any problems with Nancy or Wayne?" Flotten asked as he clicked his pen two or three times.

"Nope. None of our kids been in trouble with the law 'cept him," Harold said, his face cold as a marble floor. "We got nothing more to say to you folks. You just like sticking your noses in people's business, don't you? Mr. High-an-Mighty. Gather your stuff up now. Get. We're done here."

Escorting Flotten to the door, Harold Torgerson said, "I'm going to be real straight with you. You tell the rest of your pack too. I am not going to spend one penny, not one red cent, towards David's bail. You got that? We do not want him to come home again. Ever!"

Flotten sat in his car and made notes. He liked to do that while his memory was fresh. He dated the page, April first—fool's day, how appropriate. April's ugly in Minnesota, he thought, dull and muddy. Then he wrote:

> The Torgerson's have washed their hands of their son, David. Torgerson's parents blame others for their problems. Harold Torgerson is a bitter man, who likes to complain about government bureaucracy. Future visits would be futile.

That about sums it up, Flotten thought to himself as he shoved the yellow pad into his worn briefcase. Long as I'm in town I might as well drive over to the local police department and see if they can fill me in about the Torgerson family.

"Yup I know 'em. They're a strange lot," the desk sergeant said after Flotten showed him some ID. "Got a call one summer evening, years ago now, I could look it up for ya if you want. Someone called in—said a young boy was riding his bicycle past her house in his all-together. Patrol found him right off the bat. Kid gave his name and address: Wayne Torgerson. The officer, Bud Mytten, it was, he put the boy's bike in the trunk and took him home. Walked up to the front door, tells the parents he's got their kid in the squad. Afterwards, why, he tells me they said the boy was confused. They didn't know him from Adam.

"Bud, he goes back to the car. Questions the boy some more. Boy says, he is who he said he was and this **was** his house. Starts to cry. He lived there all right—damnedest thing…"

David Torgerson complained to Flotten too.

"My folks played favorites, blamed me for stuff I didn't do. I didn't get no free time when I was a kid," Torgerson said. "I had to come straight home from school to work in the garden or baby-sit. I wasn't allowed to go out and play like other kids was."

"How about your sister, Nancy?" Flotten asked. "Seems you fought with her a lot before your commitment."

"Nope, we mostly got along." Torgerson said.

That didn't square with the social work reports. Several of David's fights with his oldest sister, Nancy, were documented. Flotten also found a notation tucked inside Torgerson's initial psychiatric evaluation which said:

> The subject appears to have pent-up anger directed toward females. He talked at length about his resentment of Mrs. Larson, a teacher who put him into special education classes in middle school.

And then there was the long list of victims: Torgerson had been brought before the probate court for attacks on very young girls on September 19, October 20, November 5, and November 10 of 1958, and he had committed a violent attack of a ten-year-old girl on July 12, 1959, which resulted in his commitment to the state mental facility in Rochester.

In order to determine the severity of this attack, Flotten interviewed the girl's attending physician, Dr. Nesse, a popular family practitioner in Austin. The doctor confirmed Flotten's skepticism when he said, "If he'd strangled her for just one more second, she'd be dead." In addition, the victim list also included three more assaults, which occurred during Torgerson's eight-year commitment.

Flotten's comprehensive report contained details of Dr. Tyce's court ordered meeting with Torgerson, which came about as a result of the Hogan assault. Dr. Tyce stated that Torgerson was "delighted" to see him and that Torgerson "resisted" discussing the charge at hand. Instead, he wanted to tell the doctor stories about his little girl, Sylvia—just like a son wanting his father's approval would do—but Tyce held no fatherly illusion toward Torgerson. In his letter to the court, he described Torgerson as being, "a pathetic, inadequate individual who has never been able to make a living for his wife and child."

Parole agent Flotten drew a more accurate assessment of Torgerson's threat to society than Dr. Tyce ever acknowledged. His extensive report concluded:

David Torgerson seems to be saying that there was nothing really wrong with his choking of the girl (Hogan), as long as one can understand the reasons behind it. One must consider how close to death this young woman came. The defendant has shown again and again his potential to be extremely dangerous, which is not indicated by his mild and cooperative façade. This agent feels that it would be extremely dangerous to place this man on probation. I consider David James Torgerson to be a disorganized and potentially explosive person. He should be institutionalized and provided with extensive psychiatric care.

As part of the pre-sentence investigation, Judge Franke also appointed Dr. Richard Holmes, a clinical psychologist, to examine David Torgerson. Dr. Holmes administered the Minnesota Multiphasic Personality Inventory (MMPI) along with a battery of other tests. In his letter to the court, Dr. Holmes wrote: "David James Torgerson's MMPI results show potential for strong, uncontrolled emotional outbursts. Other testing outcomes suggest Torgerson can be classified as an uncontrolled and angry sociopath personality."

Torgerson was brought before the court on May 17, 1970, to hear his sentence.

Outside of the court officials and the defendant, Darlene Knutson, Torgerson's mother-in-law, was the only person who stayed to hear the trial's outcome.

Judge Franke's taut voice reverberated across the empty space. "I am concerned especially with the instances while you were a patient at the State Hospital and while working at ABC. About your advances on women. When they failed to cooperate with you, over something as simple as an act of kissing, your immediate response to their resistance was to attempt to choke them or throttle them by placing your hands around their neck.

"You had basically ten years to work your way out of this behavior pattern, which apparently you haven't been able to overcome."

Seeming to search for inner strength, Judge Franke paused and looked up at the ceiling. Rising an inch off his chair, he made no attempt to control his disdain. In a frosty voice, he continued, "**You understood** what you were doing. According to Dr. Tyce, **you knew** the nature of your acts and the probable consequences. The fact that you had this long period of treatment by an excellent hospital staff and still came off with the inability to control yourself is of great concern to me.

"For that reason, I am going to sentence you to the state prison for the maximum term under this crime of simple robbery, which is five years. I am not personally convinced that it is going to do anything to solve your problem. In fact, the opposite is true. I am quite convinced, on the basis of reading the pre-sentence investigator's findings, that if I fail to do this I would be personally responsible for the next girl that happens into your path at the wrong time. For, as **you** say, this just happened to hit me at the wrong day, at the wrong hour.

"I, for one, am not willing to assume personal responsibility for your actions in the light of your past." Settling his robe beneath him Judge Franke sat down fully and drew a deep breath.

"Therefore, you, David James Torgerson, having been convicted of the crime of simple robbery in violation of

Minnesota Statutes 609.24 and 609.17, by your plea of guilty, it is the sentence of this court that you be committed to the care, custody and control of the Commissioner of Corrections of the State of Minnesota for a period not to exceed five years. No bond having been furnished, there is none to be released. The sheriff will then deliver you to the custody of the Commissioner of Corrections at the State Prison."

"What about time served, your Honor?" Gullickson interjected. "He has been incarcerated in the county jail since the middle of February."

"There will be no credit for 'time served' counselor," Judge Franke huffed. "The reason that I deny it, to make the record specific, is that although the offense of simple robbery, with which he is charged, and to which I am sentencing him, would normally not justify this action, the attendant circumstances were, in fact, a physical assault on a girl that left her in an unconscious state and, but for the intervention of third parties, we might well have been here on a murder or manslaughter charge instead of a simple robbery charge. My great concern is that the public is going to be imperiled even at his release five years from now. I want him held for the maximum period! Okay?" Judge Franke pushed his chair back and, with a resolute gesture, scooped his papers up and exited the courtroom.

27

On June 5, 1970, David James Torgerson started serving his five-year sentence at Stillwater State Prison, a correctional facility for men located in Bayport, Minnesota. Lana Torgerson was left alone to care for their six-month-old daughter, Sylvia. The bills, the dirty diapers, getting up in the middle of the night to tend a colicky baby—all of it fell on her less than capable, restless shoulders.

The Big House, convict slang for prison, had a lot in common with a proper boarding school. Both places provided 'three hots and a cot,' adults to monitor and record each participant's progress, opportunities to learn new skills, and time to write back home, which is truly important if a fellow was lucky enough to have a girl waiting for him. And, at the end of it all, a guy might even merit a note (one that illustrates his true character) from the head administrator.

"Go ahead and get settled, David," veteran prison guard, Stefan Curia, said to Torgerson at the beginning of their in-take interview. "I'm going to help you understand how everything goes in here and then you can tell me your story. Okay?"

"Yes sir. I never been in prison before," Torgerson bobbed his head. "Nice, you helping me out—I need all the support I can get."

"Right," Curia replied. He couldn't help but notice the anxiety that spread across his newbie's face. "Everyone here starts out in what we call close custody. If you prove yourself trustworthy, you get to move up to medium, where there's more freedom. You're still locked-up though. Minimum security, that's the one you wanna shoot for, is when you can walk the grounds on your honor that sort of thing. Capish?"

Torgerson looked confused, wiped his hands on his pants.

"That's Italian for understand. I'm from Brooklyn. New York. Been in Minnesota awhile though," Curia grinned. "You just mind your p's and q's, we'll get along good."

"Yup. That's me. I ain' gonna cause you no trouble," Torgerson answered fast as a bullet. "Like I said, I been real nervous about this. You tell me what to do and it's… I'll get it done."

"How about you tell me your background, how come you here. Save me the trouble of reading this," Curia said moving a manila file forward an inch.

"Okay, sure. Everything," Torgerson exhaled. "Not much really. I been at Rochester State Mental Hospital for this girl. I grew up down in Austin, Minnesota, the home a SPAM. It's good grilled. Anyway, I needed money for my baby. I got a daughter, name's Sylvia. My wife, oh, she makes me laugh," Torgerson looked down, dropped his chin. "She's my honey. Keeps me in-line an stuff. She was the one told me to try out for the Army. It didn't work out though.

"Why I'm here is. We had them bills…This woman, I wanted her purse. She got real scared like and I just panicked. I mean, I had to shut her up. It was only natural, you know. If she hadn't yelled like that—I didn't mean to choke her, didn't hurt her none. Pressed too hard. I feel real bad. Needed money for rent, my wife, baby. That's it."

Torgerson looked up and said, "I'm here for the robbery. I did the robbery."

Torgerson's clean-shaven, baby face and honest manner carried weight with Curia. He wrote the following note about their first meeting:

> From my observations of David Torgerson, a first-time inmate, and from what he has told me, I would say this choking behavior occurs when he is with a panicky female. A situation arises, she panics, he panics and he chokes. So far he has had enough control to stop before doing any physical damage.
>
> The choking incident arose largely because of this inmate's inability to make enough money to support his wife and child. There is a long story behind it, but in a nutshell, he was desperate for money and chose to steal for an immediate solution to his problem.

Curia's assessment concluded: "Although he is not very bright, David Torgerson is a very warm, affectionate person. His great fondness for his wife is obvious. This relationship should be encouraged." Even though Curia reported Torgerson's past 'choking' behavior to the prison doctor, nothing in his file indicates he ever received psychiatric treatment while incarcerated.

"I been thinking of taking up weight-lifting," Torgerson confided to Curia during their next meeting. "But I'm scared of the homosexual wolf crowd that hangs there. I don't want to get hurt by them guys."

Curia sympathized:

> In my opinion, David Torgerson needs to be protected from aggressive homosexuals. I believe prison can do him great harm. He should be kept here just long enough to learn a trade, than (sic) he should be released. The best thing that can be done for him is to make him self-reliant. Torgerson is in dire need of vocational training and he has expressed a definite interest in learning welding. David's excitement was clear when he told me, 'Then I'd really have something.'

Torgerson's prison file contained mixed progress reports from his welding and G.E.D. instructors. One teacher said he was a "good, hardworking student," while another contended, "Torgerson is immature—a constant goof-off." Torgerson remained in close supervision for the first year. He was moved from medium custody to the minimum-security section of the prison in the beginning of 1972. During the first year of his confinement, Torgerson's wife was a faithful monthly visitor. Sometimes her mother, Darlene Knutson, rode along with her daughter on the scenic drive up to Stillwater prison. Both of them liked having the extra time to talk.

It's wonderful to be a grandmother, Darlene thought as she touched noses with baby Sylvia, who lay nestled in her lap. Despite his current situation, she had become fond of her son-in-law too. All of her girls were married now—had someone to look out for them—and she was glad about that.

Torgerson communicated with his wife through phone calls and letters. He sent this letter eighteen months after his incarceration:

> January 23, 1972
>
> Hi honey
>
> I got your letter last week & was very happy honey to hear from my little family. This is Monday the 23 all ready. This month has sure gone by fast, honey. Honey, I want you to do me a favor. I want you to send me about three dollars. I ran awful sort (sic) of money this month and I don't have any coffee or cigs untell (sic) three weeks from now. Three dollars isn't very much, honey, but it means a lot in here so if you can dig it up for the old man right away I promise I'll give you ten more kids instead of five. Ok, honey?
>
> Have you got the car fixed yet, honey? I sure hope so. Its been two months since I last seen (sic) you. I sure wouldn't want another visit like the last one. I was depress (sic) for three weeks.
>
> Loving from your husband
>
> David James Torgerson
>
> xxooxx

In their last prison visit Lana had big news for David. She was four months pregnant and the Torgersons had never enjoyed a conjugal visit.

"Suppose you noticed I'm gonna have another baby," Lana said. "I'm due in June. I hope it's a boy. We already got Sylvia. A boy and a girl. That would be nice, huh?"

"Who you been with?" he shouted. "I'll kill him." Torgerson stood halfway out of his chair, leaned across the visiting table, his face turning scarlet. The guard noticed and took a step in Torgerson's direction, motioned for him to sit back down.

"I'm not saying," Lana scowled. "None a your bees-wax! I can't stay home all the time. It don't matter none. You're the real one anyway."

It was true. No one had replaced him in her life. There were men—men who didn't mind taking advantage of a simple-minded girl: married men, drunken men, old men—men who gave her a few bucks here and there.

Torgerson's eyes misted. "How long you been steppin' out on me?"

"I ain't," Lana declared. "You shut up! I didn't come all the way up here to get yelled at. Gas cost money. Money, I ain't really got now, do I?"

On February 2nd, Torgerson simply walked away from Stillwater State Prison. He was found the next day strolling through a residential area of Stillwater, an historic tourist town on the St. Croix River, located just five miles north of the prison.

After the guards brought him back to the prison, Torgerson was placed back into close supervision for the next six months. On paper his excursion added one-and-a-half years to his sentence. In reality, his day of freedom cost him nothing. He would still be released from custody way before his five year sentence was up.

After Lana Torgerson gave birth to her second child, Johnnie, the couple communicated through phone calls and letters like these:

February 4, 1973

Hi honey

Well here it is another Monday over with, its 11:30 p.m. now. It sure did feel like winter today that wind was real strong and cold all day. I just went to bed about a half-an-hour ago and I been thinking so much about you honey that I couldn't get to sleep so here I am.

Really honey. I can't get you off my mind for some reasen (sic) today. I hope everything is all right around there. I haven't hurd (sic) from you for so long, and I do worry about you and the kids honey.

Is Bruce back from that other place yet & are they going to stay in Minnesota or move to another state? I'll sure be glad to get out of this state.

My welding is coming along fine and I took a lot of tests today. The only thing I don't like is blue print reading, but it is an important part of welding so I have to do it.

xxooxx

Lana's response began sharp as Wisconsin cheddar cheese before she melted.

February 8, 1973

Dear David

I thought I would write you a letter again, because I just got your letter today. If you think I can just jump when you say so will (sic) I can't because I have too (sic) watch every day the children & when you are up

> there you just have too (sic) take care of yourself & that is all & you know (I am) right.
>
> I'am (sic) going to see if I can get someone like Susie & Bruce to take us up to see you around the end of this month if they haven't left to where (he) is suppose (sic) to be station (sic). If you still want to see us after this letter, let me know, ok? I told you, you could call & talk to us & I will accept the charges. I got this in the mail an (sic) think you like (sic) it too.
>
> **Think a Prayer**
>
> Trust in the Lord with all your heart and he will Light the Way.
>
> This prayer came to you for good luck. The original came from the Holy Land. It was send (sic) around the world 23 times. The good (luck) has been sent to you.

A few days before he entered his work release program, Torgerson received the following encouraging note from his wife.

> Hi honey
>
> I thought I would write & answer your letter. I'am (sic) going to have my phone unlisted number & I'll know Monday what it is because that is when they going to change it ok & I'll tell you why when I see you ok? Will (sic) I have a lot of things to pack & I haven't started yet but I have too (sic) pretty soon if I want it to get done. It is a nice day

out today which is Friday. Sylvia wants to say something to her daddy.

Isn't that cute?

My new phone number is (289-3608). It is (an) unlisted number so don't loose (sic) it because you won't be able to get it, ok.

Lana

The final message found in Torgerson's file was written by Stillwater State Prison Warden, Ron Wabash. It said, "This man shouldn't be released. He'll kill someone."

Kenneth Schoen (then Minnesota's Commissioner of Adult Correction) signed David Torgerson's prison discharge order anyway, which was not all that surprising given his involvement with Dr. Tyce's PORT (Probationed Offenders Rehabilitation and Training) program: a plan that promised to save the taxpayer's dollars by releasing Rochester State Hospital's inmates back into society.

28

> She had big boobs. I wanted to touch them.

Rebecca (Becca) Rathbun was a shy, clumsy teenager who wanted to be daring. Her sister, Belinda said, "Becca would have been a rebel but she couldn't find a cause." Becca parted her thick chestnut hair, which reached past her shoulders, down the middle just like her idol Janis Joplin. Because she was big-boned and big-busted, some people mistook her to be the oldest of the Rathbun girls, instead of third in the lineup. There was no disputing she was strongest of them all. Becca could wrestle her older brother, Ross, a strapping six-footer, to the ground. Her sisters cheered each time she sat on his chest.

Just a year apart in age, Belinda and Rebecca were a lot alike. They both loved the outdoors, horses, folk music, and tie-dye shirts. Before falling off to sleep each night they shared girlish thoughts with each other in the dark. They whispered about the events of the day and trusted the other enough to disclose secret crushes. Sometimes they cried together over their parent's divorce. The loss of their father's love was hard to take and they yearned for a better future—one without Norm Anders, their mother's angry new husband.

As youngsters, Belinda and Rebecca (Becca) Rathbun loved to ride the two ponies, Dolly and Ginger. The horses had come with the farm their father was working on. Often, their sweet voices lifted over the rolling pastures of southern Minnesota when they sang call-and-response ballads such as 'The Keeper.' They always sang the first refrain in unison.

> *The keeper did a hunting go*
> *And under his cloak he carried a bow*
> *All for to shoot a merry little doe*
> *Among the leaves so Green-O,*

When they got to the chorus, Belinda called out 'Jackie Boy' and Becca responded, 'Master.' When Belinda sang, 'Sing ye well,' Becca replied, 'Very well.' Their sweet harmony floated across the pasture as they chanted the entire chorus.

> *Hey down - Ho down*
> *Derry, derry - Derry down.*
> *Among the leaves so green*
> *o-so green-o.*
> *To my hey down, down*
> *To my ho down, down.*

As soon as school let out in the spring of 1973, fifteen-year-old Belinda Rathbun accepted Lana Torgerson's offer to become her live-in baby sitter. Since Lana never yelled or got upset, it seemed like a perfect solution for both of them. A live-in babysitter gave Lana companionship during the day and freedom at night and Belinda got to run away from home.

"I can't pay nothin' regular," Lana said, sporting her typical goofy grin. "Just a couple a bucks now and then. I'm getting me a new apartment next week. You can help me move. It'll be fun."

"Sounds good to me," Belinda said. "I could use a break. I'm sick to death all the ranting and screaming going on here. If I'm at your place, Norm won't be able to pick on me anymore."

Life with Lana came with its own set of drawbacks. As soon as they woke up in the morning, Lana hustled the children and Becca into the car for another day's adventure. Lana loved to be on the move—whether from habit or necessity—and it was an effective way to avoid dealing with the system. Belinda peeled more than one note left by a frustrated social worker off Lana's front door.

"Here's another one," Belinda said, handing off the latest message. "Pretty soon they're going to cut your money off."

Lana laughed as she crumpled up the message. "I don't want nobody poking their nose in my business. Telling me how to clean-up, buy groceries, or cook. I been doing fine. Nope, don't need no help."

Belinda didn't argue even though Lana's idea of a square meal consisted of Twinkies and orange soda pop. After stocking up at the Seven-Eleven, Lana often drove over to the Coast-to-Coast store where her buddy, Dennis worked. Coast-to-Coast was Lana Torgerson's answer to car maintenance. She bought a case of motor and transmission oil there every two weeks or so. That's how she and Dennis

Rottenbury became friends. He always carried the heavy stuff out to the car for her.

"Hey, Denny, how yah doin'?" Lana chirped. "This here's my sitter, Belinda. Belinda say 'hi' to Dennis, he's my buddy."

Dennis' face lit up. He liked how Lana could talk to just about anyone. She trusted people right off, like he did. Dennis' big heart made him a sucker for a gal with a hard luck story. Occasionally, he loaned Lana fifty bucks so she could make her car payment. "It weren't nothing romantic," Dennis declared to a co-worker. "I like to help out those in need, you know. That's why I volunteer as a Big Brother."

"I stopped by to give you my new address," Lana told Dennis. "It's the top floor of a house this time. Soon as me and Belinda unpack, I'll have yah over for beer or somethun'."

Most nights Lana dropped Belinda and the kids, Sylvia and Johnnie, off at the curb close to eight o'clock, and then she zoomed off into the night. The bottle feeding, the changing of diapers and the bathing of the toddlers, all of it, fell in Belinda's lap. Living with Lana was quickly losing its allure. Belinda suffered from car-sickness and she yearned for a home-cooked meal, one without cream filling. Feeling tired and lonely, Belinda started pressuring Lana to take her back home.

"We got us a deal. You can't change out now," Lana said with a scowl on her face. "I know what. Less go over to McDonald's, get us a happy meal."

"I don't want a Goddamn happy meal. I hate your new place. It gives me the creeps," Belinda retorted. "I won't sleep there alone at night anymore. I'm going to call your worker unless you take me home. Let them find you someone else."

"Oh Belinda, no problem. I'll drop you at your Mom's house. Hold your horses. No need to yell at me, you know. I'll get you back home."

"Becca, your sister's home," Joy Anders yelled over her shoulder as she embraced her daughter, Belinda. Becca raced into the kitchen and sandwiched her sister Belinda in a group hug. Sylvia and John squealed for attention too, which prompted Becca to crouch down to kiss their cheeks.

"Johnnie you stink!" Becca said wrinkling her nose.

"Here, yah go," Lana laughed, handing over a diaper. "How 'bout you take your sister's place at babysitting? You're good with the kids. They like you."

Motioning Lana to sit, Joy uncovered a half-eaten cake, grabbed clean plates from the dish rack, and cut everyone a generous piece. Belinda opened the fridge. Real food, she thought, pulling out a left-over piece of chicken as she poured herself a big glass of milk.

Between bites of cake, Lana bragged about taking a trip over the Fourth of July to Arkansas. "You wanna ride along?" Lana asked, turning in Becca's direction. "It'll be fun. It's real pruddy there, Becca." Lana said smiling at the sweet-faced teen. "I'll take yah to the Ozarks, all of Arkansas. Dija know they call it 'The Land of Opportunity?' I looked it up. Just like Minnesota's the Land-a-Lakes—Arkansas' Opportunity."

"Nah, she don't. Leave her alone," Belinda grumbled, her mouth full of chicken. "I just got home. We need to catch-up."

"I'm a good driver, too," Lana said to Joy. "You can ask my mom. She'll say, 'Yup, that Lana, she's a good driver, a real good driver'."

Joy Anders thought about it while she sipped her coffee. "I dunno…Becca?"

I'm gonna pick-up David from his half-way house for the long weekend." Lana said. "How 'bout let Becca ride along to St. Paul this Saturday?"

"Can you take one more person?" Joy asked, suddenly thinking of her friend Leona whose daughter lived on St. Paul's East Side.

Two days later the naïve fourteen-year-old climbed into the back seat of Lana Torgerson's dilapidated family station wagon. Lana handed Sylvia over. After buckling the three-year-old in next to her, Becca held out her arms for the baby, Johnnie.

"Give him his bottle. He'll probably sleep the whole way," Lana directed as she plopped the diaper bag next to Becca. Leona Windler slid into the front passenger seat. With Lana at the wheel, they all took off from Rochester for the Twin Cities.

"Boy, David's gonna be real happy to see me. He got out a prison Monday. They let 'em out early—on account good behavior. He's a welder now," Lana bragged to Leona.

As part of his work-release program, Torgerson had started a welding job at American Hoist & Derrick in St. Paul. After his shift ended at 3:30 p.m., he returned to his half-way house. Ten minutes after he got there Lana pulled up the drive honking her horn.

"I only got a day pass," David said to his wife as he crowded into the back seat pushing the teenage babysitter,

Becca Rathbun, over to the middle. "I need to be back by 10:30. Okay, honey?"

"Sure, David," Lana laughed, happy to be driving down the road. "I got to take Leona across town. She's one of Becca's Mom's friends," Lana said to her husband as she fiddled with the radio knobs.

"Let me do that, Lana, you just watch the road kid," Leona said.

"You want to hear some country, David?" Leona asked, turning to smile at him. "This here's a good one. Johnny Cash. You like him?"

Torgerson didn't respond. He was too busy teasing the young teenager squished next to him. He tickled her feet, pinched her side, and tried to touch her boobs. Swatting his hands away, Becca's face flushed deep as Heirloom tomatoes. Embarrassed and feeling uncomfortable about what she had just witnessed, Leona gave a quick glance at Lana who was giggling and winking at David in the rear view mirror. Damn, her hubby's monkey business doesn't piss her off none, Leona decided, shrugging it off. None of my business, I guess.

Then Leona recalled Lana reading that silly ass letter out loud to her mother, Darlene, the one from some guy down in Arkansas. They had all been sitting around having coffee at Joy's table discussing the upcoming fireworks when Lana said, "I can always drive down to meet my other boyfriend if me and David don't get along." It all made sense now, Leona surmised, as she settled back into her seat. I bet David and Lana aren't going to get along for very long, she thought to herself.

29

As soon as he was settled in his St. Paul half-way house, Torgerson looked for prey. He found her in the want ads.

On Wednesday June 27, 1973, David Torgerson called Barbara Wilson in response to an advertisement she had placed in the *Minneapolis Tribune* offering her professional bartending services. He told her he was going to throw a party for a wealthy friend of his and expected one-hundred-and-fifty guests to attend. After a brief conversation, Torgerson hired Miss Wilson to come to his home in Rochester on Saturday, June 30.

The Torgersons arrived in Rochester around 6:45 p.m. on Friday, June 29, and Lana drove David straight over to the Coast-to-Coast Hardware store.

"This here's my husband, David," Lana said. "David, say hi to my best bud, Denny."

Torgerson stuck out his hand, "I just come down from the cities. Worked all week. I'm a welder. Right, honey?"

Ignoring her husband, Lana said, "Hey, Denny, wanna come over for a beer?"

"Gee whiz, that sounds swell. Wish I could. I gotta close up. How 'bout tomorrow? I get off round five."

The next day, Torgerson took his family and the babysitter, Becca Rathbun, to the local McDonald's. He ordered two happy meals for the children and a Big Mac for himself.

"What do you want, honey? You can have anything you want, honey. I'll get it for you."

Lana smiled. "Fries and a coke and one of them apple flips. Becca wants a cheeseburger, right?"

The cautious teenager shrugged. After lunch they dropped by to see Lana's mother, who lived in a well-used one-bedroom trailer. Torgerson carried a pail of wet diapers to the back door while Becca got the kids out of the station wagon.

"Hey, Mom," Lana yelled, "bring out the key to the shed. We need to use the machines."

As soon as she saw him, Darlene Knutson hugged her son-in-law, David, tight and then invited him inside.

"Well, so this is your pad," Torgerson said while watching his mother-in-law pour him a glass of lemonade.

The tiny trailer was the heart of the family: Janice had already left her children in Darlene's care for the day. They tumbled outside to play with their cousins to vie for Becca's attention. As soon as the clothes dryer hummed to a stop, Becca plopped the load of diapers into a blue plastic hamper and hauled it to a small table under the awning. "Who can hand me the most diapers?" she asked, to a hubbub of swirling hands.

Meanwhile, Barbara Wilson, the bartender-for-hire, drove into Rochester and easily found the address she'd been given. She wanted to set-up early for the Torgerson affair. A party this big's bound to lead to another, she told herself. When she realized no one was home, she scribbled a note, which included a local phone number where she could be reached, and slipped it into the door frame.

"I don' know nothin' 'bout no party," Lana Torgerson told Wilson over the phone.

"David Torgerson hired me to come down here from the cities. Do you know him?"

"Yeah, but he ain't home jus' now," Lana said with a curt clip to her voice.

"Okay, have him call me when he gets home. Tell him I'll need a couple of hours to set-up," Wilson said.

That afternoon the mercury inched close to ninety degrees.

"Let's get out of this hot house," Richard Carlson said to his wife, Janice. "I can fire-up the bike. Take you for a ride round the lake or something."

"Yup. That'll work. How 'bout we go over to Lana's new place? Mom says David come home."

As Janice and Richard climbed the duplex stairs to reach her sister's second floor apartment, they heard loud, angry voices but couldn't make out what was being said.

"Hey, David, how's it going, my man?" Richard said, in an effort to cool the situation down after Torgerson answered the door, "I got my hog downstairs. Let's ride."

When the guys returned, Becca Rathbun and the toddlers were waiting in the back seat of the station wagon. Lana sailed out the door past them with Janice right on her heels.

"Come on, David, get in," Lana ordered. "I need a couple things from Seven-Eleven."

After the station wagon pulled away from the curb Janice, muttered to Richard, "She acts like she don't want nothing to do with me now he's back in town!"

"Ah well, we better leave them alone 'cuz they only have the weekend," Richard said with a shrug. "Jump on, baby. I'll take you for a spin around the lake. We can throw a blanket down to save a spot for the fireworks before we pick up the kids from your mom's."

Having waited for her call back all afternoon, an exasperated Barbara Wilson returned to the Torgerson residence just after five since the guests were expected to arrive at seven. She rapped on the downstairs door and waited. No one seemed to be home. Confused, Wilson walked over to the next door neighbor's house.

Ginny Johnson answered the door and confirmed the Torgersons lived there. "I don't know him. The wife, she just moved in a couple of weeks now, I hear her burn rubber all the time. She comes and goes—day and night. Rowdy bunch," Ginny said. "But what are you going to do?" Wilson turned on her heel to leave and saw a beat-up station wagon pull curbside. "Guess you're in luck," Ginny Johnson said, nodding her head toward the parked wagon. "That's her."

Wilson stomped over to the car and Lana poked her head out of the driver's side window. Torgerson sat in the passenger seat staring straight ahead. He let his wife do all of the talking.

"Ain't no party," Lana said before Wilson uttered a word.

"What the hell, I can't believe it. Life's just not fair," Wilson retorted. "You telling me I drove all the way here from Minneapolis for nothing? I had to pay for the gas and I lost this whole damn holiday to boot!"

Lana dismissed her by turning to the backseat. "Becca get them kids in the house. Me and David got to talk."

Dennis Rottenbury showed up for his promised Saturday night beer around 6:15 p.m. After pounding on duplex's downstairs door, he hollered up, "Hello, it's me, Denny. Come to collect that beer."

As soon as he entered the apartment Dennis spied the babysitter doing up the dishes in the kitchen while the kids played in the living room.

"Hi, Lana here?" he asked.

"Becca give Denny his beer," Lana yelled out from behind the closed bedroom door. When she and David came out from the back bedroom, neither one was decent. Lana had pulled on her panties and slipped on her husband's white T-shirt; Torgerson appeared in his boxer shorts. His pale chest heaved as he complained to Dennis about a phone call Lana had received from some guy.

"Ah, shucks," Denny said, "lots of women—they get phone calls from strangers all the time. It don't mean anything."

"I told him that," Lana said, rolling her eyes toward heaven as she grabbed a beer for herself and handed one off to her husband.

Dennis drank his beer as fast as he could before making a quick exit.

30

Lana Torgerson –January 25 1950–June 30, 1973
Rebecca Rathbun –July 11, 1958–June 30, 1973
Sylvia Torgerson –December 14, 1969–June 30, 1973
John D. Torgerson –April 5, 1972–June 30, 1973

Three days after the Rochester sheriff's office was notified by the department of corrections that David Torgerson had skipped work-release, Lana Torgerson's disgruntled neighbor, Ginny Johnson, reported a foul odor to their landlord, Marland Fierke. As soon as Fierke's truck pulled up, Mrs. Johnson gave him an earful.

"A social worker, Dorothy Kramer is her name, I know, we talked and I got her card. She was sent over to teach that young woman how to keep her house clean. Imagine that. A mother not knowing how to clean, not having time maybe, but… and now there's this odor coming from her apartment.

"It's been real quiet there the last few days. Well, there was these goings-on Saturday afternoon. Some girl showed up thinking they was going to have a big party or something. The husband hired her to bartend but it was all a scam, a con job. I wrote her name down too, poor thing driving all this way and all…"

"Thank you, Mrs. Johnson," Fierke interrupted as he pulled his tool box from his truck bed. "I'll take it from here."

Escaping the midday heat of her trailer, Darlene Knutson walked the four blocks over to her daughter's new place. Nice having Lana and the babies living so close, she thought as she stopped to check out the mailbox. Let's just see if the welfare check came yesterday—wouldn't be good to leave that hanging around. Finding the box empty, Darlene strolled up the front walkway and saw the building owner working in the recently vacated downstairs apartment.

"Mr. Fierke? I'm Darlene Knutson, Lana's Mom."

"I'm gonna evict that damn daughter of yours if she can't clean up her act," Fierke said in response. "Her apartment stinks to high heaven. I had to throw all of these windows down here wide open."

"Golly, I'm so sorry. I don't think she's home. She was planning this trip to Arkansas," Darlene said over her shoulder as she rang her daughter's door bell.

"Nope, she's not home. Listen, I'll be glad to clean-up if you just let me in."

"I thought you had the extra key?" the exasperated landlord sputtered. "I gave her two… Oh, never mind. I'll get my ladder from the truck. The hall window's most likely unlocked."

Darlene watched as Fierke placed his ladder against the side of the house and climbed into a second floor window. Soon she heard his boots thump down the stairs.

"Go on in. I tried the knob. Apartment's open," Fierke said dismissing her with a wave of his hand.

As she climbed the steep stairs Darlene realized why the land lord was so miffed. She couldn't quite place the odor. Burnt tires? Her first husband, Vernon, had done that once. Set up a campfire inside of an old tire. It stunk to high heaven. No, this was worse. More like a pile a pig shit. Darlene sighed. Maybe Lana let some meat spoil or didn't take the garbage out before she left on her trip.

After opening the apartment door, Darlene walked straight into the kitchen to throw open the window. She pulled the garbage bag from the can and tied a knot at the top. Setting it aside, she rinsed out a pan of days old soup, tomato she thought, which had been left on the stove burner. Mold skimmed across its top. When she was finished with the dishes, she grabbed up the garbage and headed for the stairs. That's when she saw it: the body lying on the floor.

For a moment, Darlene's feet stuck to the floor as if they were frozen solid—ridiculous given the heat of the day. Her heart thumped as she ran down the stairs with the garbage bag flopping behind her.

"There's a dead man laying up there!" she screamed at Fierke through the open door of the lower level apartment. Hammer in hand, Fierke scrutinized her face. Her eyes spoke volumes. They shouted terror, nothing but sheer terror.

Fierke shot across the yard, darted up Ginny Johnson's front steps and threw open her door. Mrs. Johnson appeared, her hands covered with soap suds.

"Where's your phone," Fierke demanded. "We need the police!"

Officer William Knadel and Detective James Tuttle, all the guys on the squad called him Jimbo, were the first on the scene. When they pulled over to the curb, Fierke met them on the boulevard. He said, "Mrs. Knutson, the short woman standing on the sidewalk, says there's a dead guy upstairs. She's my tenant's mother. Stinks like hell even down here. The neighbors called to complain. Why I came over."

Even before they entered the upstairs apartment, the cops knew it was true. The stench of rotting flesh is unmistakable. It's like riding a bicycle, once you've experienced it you don't forget. Knadel and Tuttle quickly discovered three bodies. A naked adult female, with long brown hair, lay in the hall. Her legs protruded into the living room where the fully-clothed bodies of two small children were also found. Pieces of cloth covered each child's face. Their throats had been slit and their feet and hands were stubbed—toes and fingers gone. A towel was draped over the adult victim's face. Her chest had been flayed like a hapless Walleye. Knadel stood still. His face open, vulnerable.

"What kind of sick bastard would do this, Detective?" the young officer asked as his superior gloved up, carefully stepped over the bodies, and opened the living room windows.

"He cut her breasts off for Chris' sake. I sure hope we don't find them in the refrigerator or some Goddamn thing like that," Knadel said, his voice keening.

"This is no ordinary killer, for sure," Detective Tuttle exhaled. "Body part collectors—pretty rare. This autopsy's gonna be grim. I'll get the coroner and evidence techs over here and call Captain McDermott. Go down and get Mrs. Knutson home. See if she has some family to come sit with her. Tell her someone will be by later when we know what's what."

Officer Knadel descended the stairs and found Mrs. Knutson standing on the still sunlit sidewalk. The sky started to show a hint of melon. Darlene's arms were wrapped around her chest.

Sometimes people tell themselves stories they want to believe.

"I don't know who it could be officer," Darlene Knutson offered up before Knadel said a word. "My daughter's in Arkansas. She said she was going last week. I just came over to check her mail." Darlene's teeth started to chatter as she repeated, "I just came over to get her mail. The landlord, he… This is so awful."

"Yes, ma'am it is. I'm sorry but we need to cordon off the area now; the crime scene. You need a lift home? Is someone there or do you have someone you can call?"

"Oh, I'll walk. It's not far," Darlene replied, looking off into the distance. "A couple of minutes and I'll be home. I'll call my daughter, my daughter, Janice. Janice will come."

"You sure?"

Darlene nodded.

"It's no trouble to give you a lift," the uniformed cop said as he walked with her to the end of the street. Darlene patted his arm, gave him half a smile at the corner. "I'll be fine, just fine. Don't worry."

"We'll be by your house in a little while, Ma'am, when we know something for sure," Knadel said in as soothing a tone as he could muster.

The phone rang in the McDermott residence and Madeline shot her husband that look. The one that said I hope this is not work. It was.

"Gotta go, dear," Captain McDermott said as he took a last bite of Madeline's fabulous fried chicken. "Save me a big piece of that watermelon." He tousled his son's hair, hugged his little girl, and pecked the wife on her cheek before leaving their backyard picnic to hustle over to the crime scene. When he arrived, he was greeted by Detective James Tuttle.

"We have three bodies up there, Captain. The renter's name is Lana Torgerson. Her mother, ah… Darlene Knutson," Tuttle said, checking his notepad to make sure he had the name right. "Her mother was cleaning up when she saw one of the bodies. Knadel sent her home. We figure the dead woman's her daughter and the children are her grandkids."

"Torgerson, Torgerson. That name rings a bell," McDermott furrowed his brows. Other cops teased him because his eyebrows looked like a couple of fuzzy caterpillars inching up a drain sprout, heading for safe haven beyond his Brylcreamed hairline.

"I'm pretty sure we got a telex from the Department of Corrections about a David Torgerson," McDermott said more to himself than Detective Tuttle. "If I'm right, he violated his parole by failing to return from a day pass. I'm gonna call dispatch, talk to Mac, find out if the guy has a wife down here."

Dispatch told McDermott the Minnesota Department of Corrections listed the fugitive's wife's name as Rita. The addresses didn't match up either. Even so, when McDermott learned Lana Torgerson's husband had been in the Stillwater Penitentiary for Men, he quickly determined they must be one-and-the-same. This has to be the guy who had failed to return from his day pass, he reasoned.

"Knadel, give me the address you have for Mrs. Knutson. I better go talk with her," McDermott said as he slid back into his squad car. Before he had a chance to turn the ignition, a call came through from Officer Miller.

"Captain, we've got a Mr. and Mrs. Norm Anders down here at the station house wanting to file a missing person's report for their fourteen-year-old daughter, Rebecca Rathbun," Miller said. "They haven't heard from her for the past few days."

"What's her description?" McDermott asked.

"Long brown hair. According to her folks, she looks older. Could pass for eighteen. Well-endowed, I guess."

"Hold on, Miller. Let me talk this over with Knadel." McDermott turned to address his duty officer. "What's the color of hair on the adult female?"

"Brown, long."

"Age?"

"Hard to tell. Maybe late teens?"

McDermott sighed and said, "Okay." Then he spoke into his receiver, "Miller, ask the parents if they know a Lana Torgerson."

A couple of seconds later Knadel heard McDermott say, "Shit! Yup, Okay then. Put them in your squad, Miller, and bring 'em on over. I'll wait for you to get here."

When the desperate couple arrived, Norm Anders fished his wallet out of his back pocket. His fingers trembled as he handed Captain McDermott a picture.

"This here, my step-daughter, Rebecca Rathbun. Becca—the family calls her Becca. Her school photo. Last spring, she graduated eighth grade."

McDermott passed the photo over to Detective Tuttle, who took it into the house to compare with the unidentified body lying upstairs. When the detective came down he turned his back on the couple and spoke softly to his boss. "It's her."

Captain McDermott started toward the couple. This was the hardest part of this damn job, he thought, makes a guy sorry to be part of the human race. Even before he opened his mouth, Joy Anders crumpled, folded into herself. Her husband put his arms around her. Supported her. She put her head into the crook of his shoulder and let out an unrelenting sob when McDermott delivered the news that Becca was dead, and, in all probability, had been murdered. McDermott waited, watched as the husband tried to console his weeping wife. Finally, he said, "I can get a hold of minister or a priest if you like. Have him meet you at your house. Whatever you need…"

"No, thanks," Norm Anders replied, his red-rimmed eyes moist. "I think my wife's in shock. I'd like to get her to a doctor. Get something that'll help her to…"

"Good idea," McDermott said. He called out to Officer Miller, who had been standing by, and was now talking to Knadel a few feet away. "Miller, take these nice folks on over to emergency. Go in with them. Explain how things are. Make sure they get what they need at the pharmacy and then take them home."

After they left, McDermott settled back into his squad car to make that drive over to Darlene Knutson trailer. He'd tell her about the babysitter, he decided, but would keep his suspicions about the grandchildren to himself for now. They'll be time enough for that, he thought, when we know for sure.

Darlene Knutson answered Captain McDermott's knock. He took off his hat as soon as she invited him in. Darlene sat at her kitchen table looking dazed. She gestured for him to sit down, but he declined. "We've identified the body, Mrs. Knutson," McDermott said with an even tone.

"It's Rebecca Rathbun—seems she was a live-in babysitter at your daughter's."

"Oh my God, no!" Darlene cried out. She put her arms on the table and dropped her head inside the circle they made. Darlene lifted her tear-stained face and asked, "You sure? How? Why? Does her mother know? Joy's my best friend. Becca's her daughter."

"Yes Ma'am, she's been informed. Her husband, Norm Anders, they come over there. My duty officer has taken them to get her a sedative. Officer Knadel tells me you say your daughter's in Arkansas. Do you know if her husband is with her?"

"I...I'm not sure. Don't think so. He's got a new job. Welding. Up in the cities. I don't have a phone number though."

After leaving the Knutson home, McDermott radioed the station house, "Let's put out an APB on the family sedan. Possible occupants: David James Torgerson and his wife, Lana. They might be headed for Arkansas."

Before he drove a block McDermott learned a fourth victim had been discovered. Partially hidden by a bare bed positioned against the wall in the bedroom, Lana Torgerson's naked corpse had been found draped with bedcovers. She appeared to have been strangled to death. Her body was decomposed but not mutilated. As he drove back to the crime scene to talk with the coroner, McDermott called dispatch to amend the APB. "Drop the wife's name," he said. "We're just looking for the husband."

The APB would have to be changed once more. Corrections had listed an incorrect license plate, one for a sedan that had been salvaged months before. The family's current car was a rusted out station wagon. By the time her sister's body was being taken to the morgue for identification, Janice Carlson had placed her two young children into their strollers and walked with her husband, Richard, down to Silver Lake to catch the fireworks celebration. When she heard her name announced over the Silver Lake's PA system, Janice panicked. Her husband, Richard, stayed calm. He gathered up their babies and escorted his wife to the concession stand where an ambulance, standing by in case of a Fourth of a July fireworks incident, stood ready. Within minutes the Carlson family was transported to Darlene Knutson trailer. Captain McDermott's squad car was parked in front.

McDermott coordinated the notification of other close family members, and then, after the reserve officers showed up to guard the Knutson and Carlson residences, he headed for home. He planned to hug his wife, pull his children into his lap, light some sparklers, and catch the last of the neighbor's fireworks from the quiet of his backyard.

Part Four

Criminals do not die by the hands of the law.
They die by the hands of other men.
　　　　　　　　George Bernard Shaw
　　　　　　　　Man and Superman

31

As soon as I finished my freshman year, I transferred to Mankato State University, where I majored in English and psychology. During my junior year, I dyed my blonde hair chestnut brown. I often used wax paper to iron it straight—this was the decade of Joan Baez, after all. Falling past my shoulders, my hair made a natural part down the middle just like that of the dead girls—Linda, Julie, Rebecca and Becca. Had we been lined up side-by-side in a photo array, we might have been mistaken for sisters.

After graduating with a teaching degree in English in 1970, I landed a job as the eighth grade English teacher in Lake City, Minnesota. Renown as the birthplace of water skiing, Lake City stretches along the shore line of Lake Pepin, an outwash of the Mississippi and Chippewa rivers. Father Hennepin originally christened the body of water Lac de Pleurs (lake of tears) when, after being captured by the Isanti Sioux, he witnessed the tribe weep at the shoreline over the death of their chief's son. Now, sail boats dot the marina instead of canoes.

As soon as the bustle of Labor Day tourists left, I moved into a furnished two-bedroom cabin across the road from the lake. With a population under five thousand, life was quiet there—too quiet, which was why most young teachers quit before reaching tenure. Attempting to drown the boredom of small town life, I sometimes traveled to nearby Rochester to shop or dine out having no idea that Torgerson had been set free to roam those same streets.

Minnesota's April rain delivered mud. Brisk wind sucked my breath away as I hurried into work. My classroom was at the end of the original school built in the 1920's. I liked the ripple of its wood plank floors. Four seven-foot classroom windows looked out over the short alley holding the school's dumpsters. The morning sun warmed each window's deep sill, which were wide enough to hold a curled teenage body—an activity allowed by me during quiet study time.

After unlocking my solid oak classroom door, I took off my coat and put it into an unlocked cabinet holding miscellaneous school supplies. Placing the day's pile of graded papers on my ancient wood desk, I grabbed a piece of chalk and wrote April 3, 1972, on the blackboard followed by: The Diary of Anne Frank, Act II.

As the bells rang out, my students settled into their seats. Sandra Johnson waved both of her arms in the air as soon as I greeted the class. There are three types of students: green hands (students who always have their hands in the air), yellow bee's (students who pay attention enough to answer a question when called on), and desert sand (students who will forever remain lost in the dunes of time).

Sandra Johnson was a green hand.

"Yes, Sandra."

"Miss Haack, me and Mary want to know how you liked your Liebfraumilch."

'What?"

"Your Liebfraumilch. My dad owns Johnson's Liquors and Wine. He said you bought a bottle on Saturday."

"How interesting, Sandra," I said. "Thank you. Class please take out your books and turn to page 193."

Sure that I would be able to find another position in the twin cities, I turned in my resignation that very afternoon. Mom was not happy.

"Bad things happen in a big city!" she said to me on the phone that night.

"They happen in small towns too," I replied.

That summer I rented a room in the Pillsbury House, a stately Victorian located on Pillsbury Avenue in the heart of Minneapolis. The Pillsbury House imposed a curfew on its residents, which made Mom happy. Twelve young women filled the six bedrooms located on the top two floors. This was as close as I ever came to sorority life. There was only one open bed, which was how I met Ann Welhan. We shared the corner room on the second floor. We had our differences. She was brighter than I was and much better read. However, she did not possess my open, trusting nature. Ann walked with a decided limp as a result of a botched childhood surgery. Months passed before she told me her surgeon had been drunk. I had to work hard to make her my friend.

Each bedroom in the Pillsbury House came with an attached private bath. The bath Ann and I shared was larger than either of the bedrooms I had growing up in Austin. Tiny black-and-white in-laid tiles covered the floor. A regal ceramic bathtub, measuring six feet long, took up the entire interior wall. A stately pedestal wash basin nested near a latticed window; its white curtains billowed in the summer wind. Our rent was all-inclusive; the residents ate together in the very formal, first-floor dining room. Meals were served promptly: breakfasts at seven a.m. and dinners at six p.m. Snacks were never offered.

Months of communal living made me restless so I rented an old, three-bedroom house in Edina, a suburb of Minneapolis. Ann moved along with me, and Marilyn Sorenson, a former teaching colleague of mine in Lake City, joined us. By the time the following spring rolled around, I had found work as a marketing director for Anchor Inn Restaurants. Ironically, their largest establishment was based in Lake City, the small town from which I had just escaped, but I got to travel around the Midwest when the job called for it, which seemed glamorous to me.

My new boss was big about hands-on experience, so although my marketing office was located in Minneapolis, he sent me back to Lake City to see how the restaurant handled crowds during its busiest week. I arrived on June 30th and stayed through the Fourth of July. When I returned to my house in Edina on July sixth, I found Ann pacing the floor. "What was the name of that guy who attacked you when you were a little girl?" she said before I could even put my suitcase down.

"David Torgerson. Why?"

"I thought so! Is this him?" she asked, thrusting the morning paper at me.

Torgerson's face, plastered across the front page of the Minneapolis Tribune, stared back at me. He hadn't changed all that much since I last saw him. The same thick-framed black glasses covered his close-set brown eyes and he still parted his dark hair on the left side. His expression was not sinister—he looked like any average Joe from Middle America.

I was stunned. My hands shook as I scanned the headlines. I needed to sit down. After reading the full report, I realized I had been staying in a motel thirty minutes from his latest crime. He had murdered his wife, their fourteen-year-old baby sitter, his three-year-old daughter, and his wife's fourteen-month-old son. The article mentioned he left a note that said, "Don't look for me. I've gone to Minneapolis."

Minneapolis? I live on the edge of Minneapolis. Could he be in town?

I called Mom.

She told me David's mother and sister had gone into hiding because they were afraid he might come for them.

Me too.

A statewide search for David Torgerson was declared. According to news accounts, Torgerson escaped in his wife's 1963 blue-green Ford Country Squire station wagon. I figured he wouldn't get far. After all, the authorities knew the make, model and license number of the car. How long could it take for them to find and arrest him? Still, I was glad I would be traveling to Milwaukee for business in the upcoming week. At least we won't be in the same state, I reassured myself.

Taking off for Wisconsin the following Sunday, I locked all of my car doors. Since Milwaukee's a good day's drive from Minneapolis, I tuned the radio to 'The Top Forty Count Down' to keep me company. Somewhere in the middle of Wisconsin a beep, beep, beep interrupted the Carpenters top hit, 'Close to You.'

"David James Torgerson, sought by Rochester police for questioning in the July Fourth murders of his wife, two children and the babysitter, may be hiding in Madison, Wisconsin..." a radio news bulletin declared. The words echoed in my brain. My stomach turned queasy and I wondered how close I was to Madison. The newscaster continued, "A Madison police official disclosed that since early Tuesday afternoon detectives have been watching his wife's car, parked a few blocks from the main part of town. Although Torgerson has not appeared in twenty-four hours, the police believe he is still somewhere in town."

I told myself I was safe. This had to be just another absurd coincidence. It's okay, you're on a Wisconsin freeway, and he's on foot somewhere in the heart of the university town of Madison. They'll get him soon.

After spending a week working in Milwaukee, I headed for home. Torgerson's name had disappeared from Wisconsin news. No more bulletins interrupted the radio programming. I looked forward to spending the next few days in my Minneapolis office before flying out to Michigan to meet with a prospective restaurant franchisee. Five days later, while watching the news in a Detroit hotel room, I learned David Torgerson had been captured in a shopping mall parking lot in Grand Rapids, Michigan. Geeze Louise. We were both in Michigan, I thought heaving a sigh of relief. It wouldn't matter anymore, they had him now. I breathed easier and slept moderately well.

32

Susan Kay Scott

Patrol Officer Richard Osborn swung by the station house to have a cup of java with the boys before starting his Saturday shift. Weekend day duty was usually pretty calm—better than a Friday night breaking up beer parties. It would be a good time to show the ropes to a college kid. Osborn had hooked up with the ride-along program when he was a guest speaker at the college. He'd done this a couple of times before and liked it. He got to talk about the job and pass along a few pointers. Ed Weber, a Ferris College student, would be meeting Officer Osborn at eight o'clock.

He spotted her when she parked the car in the hospital lot and watched her walk inside.

Susan and Glen Scott had been married less than a year when they got shocking news: Susan had breast cancer; a bitter edict to receive at any age, harder still if you were only twenty-one. After her lumpectomy, Susan's doctor recommended daily doses of radiation therapy throughout July. On the third Saturday of July, she dropped Glen off at a motorcycle shop to buy a part for his Yamaha. After a brief kiss goodbye, Susan drove over to Butterworth Hospital for that day's appointment. She never thought to lock up her car—after all, it was daylight and her appointment wouldn't take long.

David Torgerson heard the driver's side car door open and felt the car shift under her weight as she got behind the wheel. She reached down, grabbed the seat release lever between her legs and pulled the front bench close to the steering wheel, which gave him more room to hide. The engine turned over and the car started to move.

It was two o'clock and Susan was not on her way home. Instead, she drove back to the Honda shop to pick up her husband, Glen. She pulled into the back of the lot, put her car's transmission into park, and placed her left hand on the door handle while removing the ignition key with her right hand. As soon as her car stopped, Torgerson sat up, grabbed her from behind, pressed one hand on the front of her windpipe, and began to choke her.

Susan struggled and managed to throw open her car door. Tumbling out onto the pavement screaming for help, Susan's actions drew the attention of Robert C. Boelens, a twenty-year-old parts store clerk. Thinking the woman's vehicle might be on fire, Boelens grabbed the fire extinguisher off the wall and rushed to her side. As soon as he reached Susan, Boelens reached down and helped her to her feet.

"A man, a stranger, hiding in my back seat, grabbed me around the throat," Susan said, pointing at the back of a man disappearing up Market Street.

"Are you alright?" Boelens asked. "Can you walk?"

Susan nodded as the two of them headed for the front door of the parts shop.

"Don't worry, I'll get him," Boelens said. "He won't get away. Get inside and call 911."

Boelens caught up with the suspect on Carlton, a street just south of Market. He drove his Dodge van beside Susan Scott's assailant for a short distance.

"Hey man, the police are on their way, so you might as well come back with me," Boelens said through the open passenger side window. The suspect stopped, shrugged. He seemed hesitant, milquetoast; not the kind of guy who would hide in the back seat of a woman's car. Boelens pulled his van to the shoulder, reached over and opened his passenger door. "Come on, buddy, ain't no use," he said, patting the passenger seat. "Get in. I'll just keep following you until you do."

After Boelens pulled up to the rear entrance of the Honda store with Susan's attacker sitting meekly beside him, he told a co-worker to watch over the suspect while he went inside to tell Susan Scott he had apprehended the man who attacked her. By then, Susan had told her husband, Glen about her ordeal. A police siren grew loud, retreated and resumed its wail while Susan shook in the protective cover of her husband's arms. When the Honda clerk told them he had appended the stranger, Glen Scott, his face white with rage, said, "Where is the SOB?"

A minute later, Officer Osborn, responding to the call of an alleged assault and attempted robbery at the local Honda motorcycle, pulled his squad car up to the front entrance to the store. "Weber, you stay put, keep your butt glued right to this seat. You're a civilian. Let me check this out," Officer Osborn said, as a frantic man approached his black and white unit.

"They got him—the guy who attacked my wife, Susan," Glen Scott spit out, rapid-fire as Osborn climbed out of his squad car, its lights still flashing. "He's sitting in the front passenger seat of a van out back."

Walking along side Osborn to the back of the store lot, the veins in Scott's neck became visible. "What the hell's the matter with you?" Scott shouted as soon as the accused man got out of the van's passenger side door. "My wife, my wife's at the hospital getting treatment for cancer and you scare the living shit out of her just to get a few bucks?"

"It's true, it's true. I tried to rob her," Scott's assailant admitted to the uniformed officer. "All I wanted was some money because I haven't eaten in four days. I didn't want to hurt her."

"Okay, everyone just calm down," Osborn said, placing himself between the two men. "I got this under control, sir. Go back and take care of your wife. Soon as back-up comes, I'll be in to get her statement."

After Glen Scott left, Osborn gave his full attention to the suspect. "Okay pal, Put your hands on the hood. I'm going to search your pockets now. You got anything there I should know about?"

The suspect shook his head no.

Osborn pulled out a razor, a package of Gillette razor blades, two packs of matches, two maps, and a pink bus ticket from Kalamazoo to Grand Rapids. After placing them on the hood of the van, Osborn pulled put his handcuffs and said, "Okay then, how about we start with your name, date and place of birth?"

"David Thomas Anderson."

Osborn picked up on the false note in the guy's voice right off.

"Yeah, that so? Where you from fella?"

"Mason City. That's in Iowa."

"I've heard of it," Osborn said as he guided the suspect by his elbow over to the police cruiser. "How'd you end up here?"

"Oh, I hitchhiked from Chicago to Kalamazoo. A truck driver gave me a lift to Grand Rapids."

"When were you born?" Osborn asked, opening the rear door of his black and white.

"July 16, 1943."

"Social Security number?"

"Don't remember."

"Alright," Osborn nodded. "What's your street address there in Mason City?"

"I'm not saying."

"Well, who should we notify, you know, about your arrest? Who's your next of kin?" the cop said, while placing his right hand on the suspect's head. "Duck. Don't want you to bang your head none."

While Deputy Ed Wise, who had arrived as back-up, ran a check on the name the suspect provided, Osborn went inside the Honda dealership to interview Susan Scott. After confirming the man in custody was the one who attacked her, Osborn returned to his cruiser and advised the suspect of his rights.

"I don't believe you gave us your real name, son," Osborn said as he filled out the standard I.D. form at the station house. "You just pulled a name out of the air, didn't cha, cuz you're scared, right?"

"Maybe I lied," Torgerson admitted before clamming up as Osborn transported him to the receiving room of the jail.

When booking Officer Phillips asked the suspect to provide his name, he did not respond. "We'll figure out who you are and where you live so you might as well cooperate," Phillips said.

Torgerson crumbled. He gave his full name and confessed he was from Austin, Minnesota, and then he said, a sly smile forming across his face, "I think I'm going to shock you." He bobbed his head forward, looked up at the cop and whispered, "I think I'm wanted for murder in Rochester, Minnesota."

"You think?" Phillips repeated. "Who did you kill?"

"My wife," Torgerson said. "She was going out on me. I was jealous."

"How did you kill her?" Phillips asked, looking straight into Torgerson's blank eyes.

"I choked her to death."

"Osborn, better come over here," Phillips said. "This guy tells me he killed his wife back in Minnesota."

"That, right? Okay pal, come with me while Officer Phillips here gets dispatch to check this out."

Two minutes after Osborn settled Torgerson into an interrogation room, the phone rang. Osborn rose, walked to the wall phone and picked up the receiver. "Okay. Put it through," he said. After hearing Rochester dispatch confirm David James Torgerson was the prime suspect in a multiple homicide there, Osborn pulled out a chair and looked at him dead-on.

"You found out, didn't you?" Torgerson said. "You found out that I really went crazy. Now you know why I gave you the false information."

Osborn booked Torgerson on 'Assault with Intent to Commit Robbery' for what he took as the attempted robbery of Susan Scott and then wrote a hold order on him for the four murders that took place in Rochester, Minnesota.

After showering and eating dinner, Torgerson was brought back for questioning. Michigan Detectives Lieutenant Dougan and Captain Osborn took the interview.

33

In Grand Rapids, Michigan, David James Torgerson made a voluntary confession to Kent County Sheriff's Department detectives Dougan and Osborn on July 24, 1973.

"Could you tell Captain Osborn and me the events that led up to the murder of your family?" Lieutenant Dougan asked Torgerson at the start of their first interview.

"Okay," Torgerson said, scooting his chair forward. "I called my wife, Lana, about 8:00 a.m. Saturday, June 30th, to tell her I was taking the bus to Rochester. I was on work release from Stillwater State Prison and I was going to go home for the weekend. I mean until 10:30 p.m. I had to be back at the halfway house then. I arrived in Rochester about noon.

"I went over and seen Lana about, I don't know, it must have been about mid-noon or something like that and I seen them. I don't know if it was her boyfriend or not but a man left the house and she was with him. Now that I think of it, I don't know if it was her boyfriend or not. It could have been just a friend.

"I guess she got a lot of friends and they helped her out—but at the time I thought this must be the one. She was going out on me and she had told me that she was going to wait. She had a baby with another guy before my release from prison and I thought this was him.

"Anyway, I went over and we talked and we were in bed together, having relations, and I asked her who the father of the baby (John) was and she wouldn't tell. We had an argument and I just kind of went berserk, I guess. I started choking her and when I let go she wasn't breathing.

"Then the babysitter she came in and she screamed. I did the same to her. And then the kids were screaming and hollering and everything. I let go of the babysitter, and I don't know by that time, I didn't really know. I wasn't in my right mind. I grabbed a knife and apparently stabbed them and after that I really can't remember too much more."

"Okay after you strangled the babysitter… then what took place at that time?' Michigan's Kent County Sherriff's Lieutenant James Dougan asked.

"I think I mentioned about the children."

"The children were screaming, is that correct?"

"I guess. I stabbed them, and I don't know, I just can't remember much after that. I remember going to Madison in the car."

"Okay, where did you get the knife from to stab the children?"

"In the kitchen."

"And at that time you stabbed the children, can you remember which one of the children you stabbed first?"

"I think it was Johnny."

"Is Johnny the younger of the two children?" Dougan asked.

"That was the baby, yes. That's what the whole argument was about, was him."

"Okay, then the last one you cut was Sylvia? Do you recall where you left the knife at?"

"Not at this date, but I presume on the floor. I didn't take it with me anyway."

Dougan pressed for more information and Torgerson said, "I remember getting into the car and ending up in Madison, Wisconsin. Then I went to Madison, and then on to Milwaukee, and then from Milwaukee to Chicago, which I stayed about two weeks. I washed dishes there and lived in a hotel. Then I went to Kalamazoo, Michigan, stayed there one night at the Kent Hotel, then I came to Grand Rapids, Michigan, and this is where I got caught."

"Hold up a minute, David. Let's go back to Rochester," Dougan said. "Can you tell me how long you stayed at the scene? I mean how long did you stay in the house after?"

"Oh, it was a few hours. I made some soup. Figured on what to do and stuff." Having conferred with Rochester police prior to this interview, Dougan knew Torgerson used a large carving knife to cut off the babysitter's breasts and that he had also cut off the children's fingers and toes with a paring knife.

"So what happened after you killed them?" Dougan asked in a cajoling voice. "Did you do anything to the bodies?"

"I can't remember too much more now. Like I said I wasn't in my right mind," Torgerson replied, as nonchalant as if he were ordering a vanilla milkshake.

Three days later Torgerson asked to speak with the Michigan detectives again. After Lieutenant Dougan read Torgerson his rights, he handed Torgerson a pen. "By signing this statement, you are stipulating that you understand your constitutional rights and want to make a voluntary statement."

After Torgerson signed his name, Lieutenant Dougan turned on the tape recorder. He stated all of their names as well as the time and date for the record.

"Okay, David, we are responding to your request to talk with you. Is that correct?"

"That is correct," Torgerson said, sitting erect in his straight back wooden chair.

"At this time neither Captain Osborn nor myself really have any idea what all will be covered. So we are going to give the microphone to you and just let you tell your story. Is that all right with you?"

Torgerson nodded.

"David, you need to say yes for the record," Dougan instructed.

"Okay. Yes. I am going to start way at the beginning, something like about when I was ten years old. I had a pretty good childhood but ten seemed to be the turning point so I am going to start there. I started getting these feelings of hate, of women. I don't know what the reason was at the time and I still really don't, but for some reason I had a real hate for women and I would go down the street and see one alone and probably hit her. I finally got caught doing this and I ended up at the Saint Mary's Hospital for observation over in Rochester.

"In the summer of 1968, I got one of these," Torgerson paused, shook his hands and arms to show something was taking over his body. "I was wandering around Rochester and went into the Kahler Hotel Parking Ramp and there was this—it was on the top floor and this woman came out, she was in a white uniform, white pantyhose, and white shoes. She had light brown hair and I choked her to death."

Torgerson's voice was flat, as if hair color and strangling a human being to death were equivalent.

"How old would you say that woman was, do you know?" Dougan asked keeping a steady gaze.

"About twenty-nine or in her early thirties," Torgerson replied, adjusting his glasses. Dark curls fell across his forehead. His round cheeks and smooth chin made him seem closer in years to a teenager than a man who had just celebrated his thirtieth birthday.

"I left no finger prints," Torgerson couldn't resist bragging. "This other personality that takes over, believe it or not, is quite intelligent. I mean it's cunning. It knows what it is doing."

Attempting to look contrite, he looked down, shook his head. "It's just not me. I mean not like I am right now."

Looking at his timid facade, it would be easy for an ordinary citizen to find him incapable of such horrific violence, but Osborn and Dougan knew better than to judge a perpetrator by his cover.

"Let me see so I can describe it," Torgerson lifted his eyes toward the ceiling, "Her head was towards the steps, there was some steps there, and it was right by the elevator. That is about all I can give you. As far as I know when I left she was dead because I am sure she wasn't breathing."

"Are you sure she wasn't breathing?" Dougan repeated Torgerson's comment, encouraging him to provide more details. It worked.

"There was this, kind a hissing sound coming from her. It wasn't like breathing. It was just like air was escaping, you know. I can remember these things but there is just nothing I can do about them," Torgerson said, shrugging his shoulders.

Dougan shifted in his chair, gave Osborn a side-ways glance, and then cleared his throat before asking, "Did you get involved with any type of a sexual encounter with her?"

"No, it was just pure hate."

Silence blanketed the small room.

Torgerson drew a breath and continued, "January 1969, I was in Minneapolis and I was staying at the Y. The welfare was helping me out at the Y and I stayed there, I think it was about a week or two, and my intention was to find a job there and everything, which I was looking for.

"Then all a sudden this, whatever you want to call it, took over and I got all sweaty and shaky and out I went and I ended up at an apartment. It was on Chicago Street or Avenue in Minneapolis. I went into this old looking apartment building."

Osborn interrupted. "Can you describe the apartment building?"

"No," Torgerson replied. "It was an old brick building. As you go in on your left there would be mailboxes. Then you go through another door, kind of a double door thing, there would be a phone booth on your right."

"A phone booth?"

"Yeah, there was a glass box there, mounted on the wall, with a bunch of keys for all the apartments."

"An entry way?" Captain Osborn prompted.

"Yup, an entry way," Torgerson nodded in agreement. "There was these old wooden steps. You would go up them and there would be these steel doors on the top of each level. You would go through these doors and there would be apartments. I went to the top one. Way up and way down on the end there was this apartment.

"I had looked on the mailboxes and it belonged to a Linda something. I knocked on the door. This was about 10:30 or 11:00 at night, something like that. I knocked on her door. She answered it and asked what I wanted," Torgerson said, sitting straight in his chair again. "I think I told her I was looking for somebody else in the building. Then as she was turning away, I grabbed her throat. We were in the kitchen and she went down. She didn't struggle really too much. She went out right away. Next, I went and looked around the apartment. I left her in the kitchen," he said.

Dougan lifted his chin, tipped his head, and raised one eyebrow inviting Torgerson to continue his story.

"You go through the kitchen and on your left would be a bathroom, on your right would be the bedroom and kind of a living room combination. There was a bunch of clothes in there and a whole bunch of stuff, bundles of stuff.

"On her bed was a purse, a shiny purse like patent leather, you know. Her billfold, I can't remember…It was black, but I don't know if it was patent or not. I emptied that out, the purse out, I mean the billfold out, and then I went into the bathroom, filled it up with water—the bathtub.

"I picked her up and put her into the bathtub. I am trying to visualize all of this," Torgerson said. He licked his lips as he tilted his chair back, lifting its front legs off the ground an inch. "There was a bunch of clothes hanging around in the bathtub. They was over the edge of the bathtub and inside it too. She had on blue pantyhose and a brown sweater; I think it was a turtle neck. I think she had, I think it was a brown skirt, she had on.

"Anyway, I took off the sweater because I was going to use the sleeve to strangle her with and I left that around her neck when I put her in the bathtub, loose though, because she was already dead."

"You choked her with your hands?" Dougan said. "When you first saw her, did you choke her with your hands?"

"Yes."

"Killed her?"

"Yeah, right," Torgerson said, planting his chair back on the ground. "I took her shoes off. I can't remember what color hair she had. She had dark eyes though—they were dark, awful dark. She was short. That is all I can remember right now."

"Did you follow this girl, this Linda, into the apartment that day?"

"No, I didn't follow her. I didn't know her at all. Like I said, this thing just comes on me and I go out an look for somebody."

"You went out and looked for her"? Lieutenant Dougan asked, keeping his voice steady, emotionless. "You didn't see her before she came to the door and opened it up?

"No. It was just that quick, I mean it's ah…" Torgerson said, his voice trailing off.

Dougan scooted his chair forward, offered a smile.

"The next one was also 1969," Torgerson continued. "That was in the summer. I think her name was Julie. It seemed like she said that. That is what she said. Like I said, this took over again, and I was walking this night looking for one again and went by this old house. I think the house was on a corner…

"Corner of what? Where are you at?"

"In Minneapolis. Both these last two were in Minneapolis."

"You mean the one you just told about and this one or this one and the next one?" Dougan asked, feeling as if he was losing count.

"The one I just told you about and this one. She was in the window there writing a letter and I went up to her and started talking. I think I left some footprints in the dirt there because the dirt was quite soft. I'm sure they must have something, they must have checked that."

"What time of year was this?"

"This was in the summer, yeah," Torgerson said nodding. "I am sure I left footprints there because the ground was soft. That is the only thing I didn't cover up. I always wiped off finger prints and stuff. Like I say, this personality was awful smart. It was probably crazy but it knew what it was doing. You know, it was cunning." Torgerson shrugged and shook his head as if he was in disbelief, and then sat up tall. "She asked me to come in and have a beer so I accepted, you know, right away. I went in, we had a beer. I can't think of what kind it was, it was in these larger cans, I think it was 16 oz. cans and we sat at her table there, it was a small table, kind of a small kitchen.

"She had a radio going, it was in kind of a corner there by the refrigerator and then we went into the living room. As you walk out of the kitchen, I think it was on your right, there would be dresser drawers. Anyway, we sat at the table, it was kind of a big wooden table there, and she was telling me about herself and showed me an album of her family pictures. She had a high school graduation picture of herself; she was smiling. By this time it was getting to be about twelve o'clock, I remember."

"Twelve o'clock at night?" Osborn asked.

"Uh huh, at night. And then the reason we found out, we listened to the radio and the radio said that. Then she said she had to get up early, about six in the morning.

"There was one thing that might be important. There was a kind of garbage thing over in the corner. I think it was in the kitchen. It was full of beer cans. I asked her about them and she said her boyfriend was there. I guess and they were drinking a lot. It was full of beer cans. Anyway, she said she had to get up early and that I had to go.

"When she turned her back on me, I grabbed her from behind. This is the first time I grabbed one from behind. I had my right hand in front of her throat and my left one in the back," Torgerson said, drawing his hands together to demonstrate his action. "And that is the way she died then. I left her on the bed. This is the first one I took any clothes off. I didn't have relations with her, I just took her clothes off and she had wet them, they were all wet. I remember that and I left her on the bed, naked like that."

"Was she completely naked or did she have some clothes on and some off or what?" Dougan asked.

"No completely nude. She had on white slacks. That just came to me."

"She was wearing white slacks previous to this?"

"Yes. I took off these white slacks. I don't remember what she had on top. Linda, I believe, had a black brassiere on, kind of a lacy thing. Anyway, this Julie, from what I can remember her name was, I think it was her name. She had light brown hair, I believe. She was kind of stocky. There really isn't much more I can remember on that.

"I went out the back door. You had to go through a screen door. I remember closing it. I went down some steps, made a left. At the corner there I made a right and walked down to Lake Street."

"Down to Lake Street? Was this a big apartment building? Or what was this, where was this at?"

"In Minneapolis, on Twenty-Fifth Street, and that was all of that one. I left there about three O'clock."

"Three in the morning?"

Even though Dougan was weary, he continued to repeat what Torgerson had just said. Police interrogation 101: repeating what a suspect says. It makes him feel heard, understood, and that always made them talk more. After more give and take about Julie Merhman's apartment building, Torgerson said, "I always have a drink after this. I don't know why, but I do. I have a few beers or something: after, not before."

Next, Torgerson confessed to Rebecca Hanson's murder.

"All right, then there was this girl, Rebecca. I followed her in when she went upstairs. She had dark hair, dark brown hair, real long and thick. Now, I don't know if it was a wig or not, but it was real long and thick, dark brown.

"And she went to the top floor, way up to the top. The steps were real wide and she went down to the end, there was a doctor's apartment there. I remember glancing at it as I went by. And she went to the apartment at the end of the hall on the right and some guy lived on the left. I remember I seen his name there too.

"She was already in the apartment. I just followed her up there and seen her go in. I went back down stairs and came up the side way and when I got to the apartment I knocked. I was going to do the same thing as Linda but nobody answered. Apparently, she went someplace for a few minutes because then I took a screwdriver out of my pocket."

Torgerson took a moment to think up a reason for having a tool. "I had been fixing the car earlier so I had the screwdriver. I pried the door open."

After sharing a detailed account of the arrangement of the rooms in Rebecca's apartment and the furniture inside, Torgerson continued, "I went into the bedroom, she wasn't in there by the way, and hid behind the door that was right by the dresser with a big mirror on it and a bunch of cosmetics on the dresser and then she walked in.

"She put her purse on the couch, because I could see through the door you know, through the crack. She walked into the kitchen and then she put her coat away. No, she put her coat away and then she walked into the kitchen." Torgerson wanted to get all of the details right. He wanted to make sure the detectives knew he was really there—that he was the devious killer no cop could catch. And, like all serial killers, he wanted to massage the details in his mind. He had done it a thousand times.

"She came into the bedroom and she had on a blue uniform, which I recognized as a Mayo Clinic uniform. And then I came up behind her, grabbed her somewhat the same way I did Julie. She got away but then she went down. She started going down on this dressers' drawers, kind of pawing at 'em.

"I got her again when she was on the floor and her hair was in her face and everything. I was choking her and she was on her back. And then, of course, she died." Torgerson drew a breath before giving the two detectives a shy look. He dropped his hands into his lap, looked at them adding, "I hate that word."

Captain Osborn stood, shook his right leg, walked in a small circle behind his chair, and sat back down. Dougan saw Osborn clench his fingers twice before folding them together on the table. He knew his partner was fed up, seething inside. They both fixed their eyes on the blank wall just above Torgerson's head and listened passively as he continued with his tale of senseless murder.

"Then I put her on the bed but I didn't undress her. I put her on the bed and took her shoes off and put them by the bed together. Course, I wiped the finger prints off. I always wiped the finger prints off.

I went into this closet and there was a red brick in there. Why there was a red brick in the closet, I don't know. I hit her with the brick. It was several times over the forehead," he said, demonstrating this action. "She was already dead though. Now this red brick—maybe it was a souvenir from their home or something—I put it back in the closet afterwards."

Rebecca Hanson's sister, Bonnie, had dogged the Rochester police to no avail about how that red brick ended up in their closet. Most likely, Torgerson picked up the brick from the side of the Rebecca's apartment building when he went back down the stairs after following her inside the first time. He must have decided he needed another weapon in order to overpower his five foot two, 115 pound teenage victim.

"There was TV coverage of this," Torgerson informed the detectives. "It showed quite a bit of the apartment on TV. Now, I could have picked some of this up from the television coverage, but the story about the red brick... well only the killer would know about that. This is the first one that wasn't put down as a murder or homicide because I started up her bed. She had blue sheets. The TV coverage wasn't in color. So that proves it was me."

"Rebecca had blue sheets?" Dougan repeated.

Torgerson took the bait.

"She had blue—yeah…there was a black purse on the end of the bed. It might have been hers or her sister's. That is another thing that the TV didn't pick-up. There was several clothes in the closet. The thing was jammed with clothes. I remember one skirt in there that was made from brown leather. It just attracted me, it looked like something my wife would like, you know.

"They thought that she had died from smoking cigarettes, I guess. There was no ashtray on the bed, there was no cigarettes on the bed, her red purse was the one with cigarettes in it and that one was in the living room, so I don't know how they came to that conclusion."

After Torgerson admitted he stole $10.00 from Rebecca's purse, Dougan turned the questioning back to the use of the brick in the commission of this crime. Responding to whether Rebecca's head was crushed in, Torgerson explained, "Oh no, her head it didn't leave no bruise. It didn't break the skin—it was flat. No, sir, it didn't hurt her. It was right like this here: it was just thump, thump, thump that is all it did. I don't know why I hit her with it, but I did put it back in the closet though."

Osborn noticed the muscles in his partner's jaw twitch. After working together for the past five years, he knew what rolled through Dougan's brain. He could almost hear him mutter, 'Such a nice guy, cleaning up after himself like that'.

"She had a phonograph in the living room. There was a TV in the living room. Let's see—there wasn't much in the refrigerator, very little in the refrigerator. I was going to get something to eat. Imagine eating after something like that," Torgerson sighed, then picked up his story a second later. "I started the fire before I left. I put the brick back and went out the door and that was that."

"You set the apartment on fire?"

"Yes. Her bed."

"You set her bed on fire?"

"Yeah, she was dead by then though."

"I don't believe that you mentioned that before," Dougan said. "I think maybe you are getting ahead of yourself or something…"

"Oh, I can see why you was wondering why they thought it was an accident. I can't really see how come they come to a conclusion like that either. Apparently, she was pretty well burnt-up, you know. I left the apartment, went home and had dinner. I always have a drink after this, I don't know why, but I do. I have a few beers or something. After, not before hand," Torgerson emphasized again, as if this somehow made him less culpable.

"And then I seem to come back to it. I don't know how I come back to it. It might be after I do the thing or maybe it is on the way out or what, but I come back."

Detective Dougan asked, "How did you set Rebecca's bed on fire?"

"With matches. A squirt of lighter fluid."

"What part of the bed, or where?" Osborn interjected. "Did you use any papers or anything like this to help get it going?"

"No, just the sheets. It would be down towards her hips where I started it. It would be—she was on the side. Not the one toward the wall. She was on the side where…I was leaning over her there, you know, the side of the bed as you come in the bedroom.

"There was a telephone on the bed stand. I think it was a colored phone, I can't remember what color. It rang once, but of course I didn't answer it. I wasn't going to say, 'Hi this is your friendly'—ah, you know. This was toward the evening. It was close to six o'clock. I know that because I remember getting home and it was on the news and stuff. I was married at the time and we just had a baby too, in December.

"This was January. That was in 1970. Now, I usually don't go this close together with these. For some reason, I don't know, but for some reason I got the urge to do it again, just a month afterwards. Usually, ah—it is quite a ways apart, as you noticed."

Captain Osborn and Lieutenant Dougan barely had enough time to keep count. Calculating the time-line would have to happen much later.

"I went out again," Torgerson boasted. "This time I met another girl. Her name was Ann Hogan. It was cold, it was real cold. I stopped her and asked if there was any apartments listed in Rochester—apartments around where we was standing—for rent. She said not that she knew of and then she said, 'Well, I've got to go now, I live right here,' so I asked her, "would it be all right if I stayed in the hall and read this paper? I had a paper with me, see.

"After we went into the hall she invited me into her apartment and then she went to her bedroom. There was some time lapse here, but I am not going to go into that," Torgerson said, attempting to look mysterious. "Eventually, she went into her bedroom while I was still reading the paper. And then I followed her in there. I was just bringing my hands up to her throat when she screamed. This is the only thing that saved her. She screamed and her girlfriend ran, apparently she had a girlfriend right next door, and she ran down the steps and out across the street. About three minutes later, three guys come in and they asked me what I was doing. I told them I was just there to rob her.

"Now to show you how, I suppose you can use the word cunning again, how cunning this personality was, it came up with this robbery bit. I went in there, of course, with the reason that I mentioned before. And the police came then and they asked me a bunch of questions. Ann, she was just about—she was real close—almost dead. By that time I could just about tell when they were almost gone and, I mean, she was real close.

"So it wasn't a matter of just a simple assault or nothing. If they wanted to they could have got me with attempted murder, because it was that, but I talked them out of it. I got them convinced that it was robbery.

"When she screamed, I panicked and all this kind of stuff. I went to the police station and made a statement. They charged me with simple robbery. They dropped the charge of assault and everything. They knew what my record was and they should have known right then and there that it wasn't no simple assault, but it went down on the books as simple robbery. Then I went to Stillwater State Prison for almost three years."

There was never any hint of remorse in Torgerson's confession. Not from the bad guy that took over his will and made him kill innocent girls (girls who were strangers to him) nor from the good guy that sat before the Michigan police. Neither of them ever showed any sign of regret, shame or sorrow. But then sociopaths never do.

After Torgerson was removed from the interrogation room, Lieutenant Dougan said to Captain Osborn, "I'll contact Rochester about Rebecca, the girl he burned up. You call Minneapolis. See if they have a couple of unsolved murders from 1969. Have them look up any suspicious deaths for girls named Julie and Linda."

As soon as he hung up from Dougan's call, Roger Stai, Rochester's Chief of Police, drove his blue sedan over the rolling hills of Fillmore County to the simple country lane that led to the Hanson family farm. Chief of Police Stai found Rebecca's father in the barn tending to his cows. The cruel news knocked him backwards. "I liked it better the other way," Mr. Hanson said to Rochester's' chief of police as he threw down his pitch fork on the hay mow. Stai saw the farmer's shoulders slump as he walked toward the house to tell this horrible news to the rest of his family.

Rebecca Hanson's face had been so badly burnt her parents had closed the casket for her funeral. Not being able to view Rebecca's body made it harder for her younger sisters to accept she was really gone. For years, Rebecca returned to them in their dreams with a big smile on her face. Their dreams were so vivid and so clear; so desired they felt real. Then, soon after waking, it would hit them all over again: Rebecca would never be back.

When Officer Miller told Charlotte Jarrett her attacker had been found, she crouched down, put her arms around her dog and sobbed into the ruff of his neck. Riley, a seventy-pound German shepherd, a gift from Charlotte's second husband, had been her constant guardian for the past four years.

After Minneapolis Detectives Hansey and Shoemacher knocked on their respective doors, the Merhman and

Wandrus families found small comfort for their losses. It took decades of tireless effort from Julie Merhman's baby sister, 'Loupot,' to change 'the cause of death' notation on her sister, JuJu's death certificate. On June 20, 2007, Hennepin County's Chief Medical Examiner, Dr. Andrew Baker, finally listed **Asphyxia** as the cause of death with **homicide** as the manner.

34

The press coverage of Torgerson's murderous rampage was extensive. Newspaper reporters crawled all over the story once they learned David Torgerson had been released from Stillwater State Prison after serving less than three years of his five-year sentence. When reporters found out Torgerson killed his family on a day-pass granted after one week's stay at Minneapolis Salvation Army Men's residential center, they scrutinized the system's missteps and grilled the public officials deemed responsible, which included: Tom Dowdle (Torgerson's work release supervisor); Leon Linder (Chair of the Minnesota Parole Board); Kenneth Schoen (co-founder of the PORT program in Rochester and Minnesota's current Commissioner of Corrections); and D.P. Mattson (Rochester's prosecutor).

In a contentious press conference, Dowdle described Torgerson as a model prisoner to a throng of reporters. "I talked to Torgerson before he started the program and then met with him on a daily basis. There were no indications anything was wrong," Dowdle contended. "He did a good job, and everything seemed to be getting back together for him."

"Sir, can you tell us why he was given a weekend pass so soon?" a *St. Paul Dispatch* reporter yelled out from the crowd. "Don't most parolees have to earn such a reward?"

"He was turned down for his first request of a full weekend furlough," Dwodle responded. "New members of the program are not given this privilege their first weekend. Instead of the full furlough, Torgerson received 'a daylight-hours pass,' which required him to return by 10:30 p.m. that evening."

"Yeah, but he didn't, did he? Torgerson showed up after curfew," another reporter said. "My source at the halfway house tells me he showed up at one-thirty in the morning. How'd he get a pass for Saturday when he didn't follow the rules on Friday?"

"I'm not sure how it happened, but he was given another daylight hours pass the next morning, on Saturday," Dowdle acknowledged as a flash bulb went off.

"And that was the last we saw of him. After I learned Torgerson failed to report to work the following Monday, I asked Leon Linder, the Adult Correction's Chairman, to issue a warrant for his arrest," Dowdle explained as he handed off the microphone to Linder.

In his role as commissioner, Linder signed Torgerson's work release agreement which stated, "Whereas, the said Commission, after careful consideration, believes that there is a reasonable probability that said individual will lead a law-biding life, and believes further that the release of said individual on Work Release is compatible with the welfare of society, the Minnesota Parole Board grants work release to David Torgerson."

"Can you tell us why Torgerson was granted early release?" a reporter demanded. "I talked with a court house staff member from Rochester. She told me Judge Franke gave Torgerson the maximum sentence of five years and that he stipulated Torgerson should serve his full term. What do you have to say about that?"

"There were no misconduct reports on his record prior to release," Linder responded. "I think they were going on the theory that a transition period was essential. The parole board received a unanimous recommendation from the prison classification committee to release him. We didn't want to just thrust him upon society." Linder switched the microphone to his left hand so he could push his damp hair off his forehead. With the microphone back in place, he continued, "We knew Torgerson had problems and emotional difficulties in the past and there was some potential for problems in the future. As a result, we felt it would be best to have him under a closely supervised and controlled program.

"Mr. Torgerson hoped he could re-unite with his family and, apparently, Mrs. Torgerson was thinking along these same lines since she hadn't started divorce proceedings," Linder said while pulling a handkerchief from his suit pocket. He mopped his brow and shot a sharp look into the crowd of restless reporters. "I think it is possible to understand Torgerson's vengeful response. Why, it's just natural—any husband would be upset about such a situation."

Over two hundred newspaper articles were written about Torgerson's early release and the ensuing tragedy. None of them ever mentioned Dr. Tyce or the petition that released Torgerson from Rochester State Mental Hospital. No reporter ever asked Dr. Tyce about his failure to recommit Torgerson after his attack on Anne Hogan. Most of the heated news accounts focused blame on Minnesota Corrections Commissioner, Kenneth Schoen, and Olmsted

County Prosecutor, D. P. Mattson. Both men were adamant the other was responsible for the system's failures.

In response to growing public criticism, Dr. Tyce's PORT Program co-hort, Kenneth Schoen, asserted the parole board acted responsibly. According to a *Minneapolis Star Tribune* article Schoen said, "The system is being criticized for letting Torgerson out too early, but would he have been any less dangerous if we had released him later? It is irresponsible for people to criticize the Corrections Department for failing to take action.

"If Rochester's officials feel Torgerson should have been imprisoned longer, they should have prosecuted him on a more serious charge. Prison is essentially a place to do time. It is in no way equipped to provide psychiatric care," Schoen said, casting a thinly veiled accusation toward the prosecutor's office. "Stillwater has only one part-time psychiatrist. If you want to know why Torgerson was not getting psychiatric care, you better ask the people who sent him to prison. When the public safety is violated by a man in the criminal justice system, then the system should re-examine what it has done."

Prosecutor Mattson fired back in the *Rochester Bulletin*: "Torgerson's mental history was not made available to the prosecution until after his conviction. The Department of Corrections, which had Torgerson's mental history and prison record, is responsible for failing to provide for public safety. If they wanted to, they could have initiated proceedings to have Torgerson committed to an institution for the criminally insane," Mattson charged. "It is the Correction Department's responsibility to put him in the proper institution. It is obvious that the parole board failed to read Torgerson's record after he was convicted. The parole board is becoming too lenient in balancing the rights of individuals with the rights of society."

None of this spurious rhetoric turned into system change.

35

The day after Michigan's Kent County prosecutor, David Kamm, announced David James Torgerson confessed to four murders in Rochester Minnesota, Kenneth Schoen issued a warrant from the Minnesota Department of Corrections seeking Torgerson's remand to prison for violation of his work release program. Torgerson was returned to Minnesota on August 11, 1973.

Even though Torgerson confessed to the killing of his wife, two children, and the babysitter, a grand jury indictment was needed in order to file first-degree murder charges against him. Rochester's Grand Jury convened to hear the evidence against him on August 20, 1973.

After two days of Grand Jury testimony from twelve witnesses, David James Torgerson was indicted on four felony counts of murder in the first degree (murder with premeditation) and four felony counts of murder in the second degree (murder without premeditation) for the deaths of Rebecca Rathbun, Sylvia Torgerson, John Torgerson and Lana Torgerson. An additional count of manslaughter in the first degree was added to Torgerson's indictment for the murder of his wife because his murder of her was alleged to have been committed in the heat of passion. No charges were ever filed on behalf of: Rebecca Hanson, Julie Merhman, Linda Wandrus, or Charlotte Jarrett.

Torgerson's first hearing, which took place on August 23, 1973, established that he was indigent and therefore had the right to be represented by a court appointed attorney. Presiding Judge Russell Olson appointed Lawrence T. Collins to act as defense counsel and D.P. Mattson represented the State of Minnesota against Torgerson for the second time.

"I want you to know the attorney that is appointed within reason will be one that meets your approval," Judge Olson told Torgerson. After Torgerson acknowledged to the court that he was satisfied with having Collins represent him, the grand jury's four murder indictments were read into the record. Torgerson was remanded into the Sherriff of Olmsted County's custody. The date of the next hearing set for a week later. On that date, defense counsel Collins moved to defer the proceedings in order to have Torgerson's mental health competency assessed.

"Well, your honor," Prosecutor Mattson said, "the State would object. If there is a question of insanity at the time of the commission of the crimes, this court should have the authority to resolve whether or not he was mentally ill and should be with the criminally insane at St. Peter."

Turning to the defense table, Judge Olson asked Collins to clarify his intention.

"I am not asking the court to make a determination about the defendant's mental competency. I just want to postpone the hearing until such a finding can be made."

While denying defense counsel's motion to defer, the judge left the option to file for civil commitment proceedings open. After Torgerson entered his plea of not guilty on all counts, Collins asked for a thirty day extension. "This will afford the defense enough time to ask for a change of venue and to employ a psychiatrist, Your Honor."

The motion was granted.

The state introduced a list of forty-two items the prosecution intended to use as evidence at trial, including evidence taken from the crime scene, the stolen automobile, and the statements made by the defendant in Michigan.

Judge Olson asked if the defense would be requesting a hearing to determine the admissibility of the prosecution's items of evidence. Collins said he needed more time to make that decision.

"Alright then," Judge Olson said, "please note that the defense will be required to state its intentions for the record at the time of our next hearing, which I am setting for one week from today on September 6. Now, is there anything else today? The bond matter is the same, that is, there was no request for bond and there is none today."

"Your Honor, I am making a motion that bail be set at this time," Collins responded.

"Oh, you are?" Judge Olson said.

"Yes, your Honor," Collins said with a poker face.

"I decided last week I would not set bond unless the defendant made such a request," Judge Olson said.

"I am making that request now," Collins asserted. "I think that he has a right to have bail set. I am aware of the various holds that would tend to preclude his release, but I think that is a separate and distinct from the matter of setting bail. I think that it should be set at this time."

Judge Olson set Torgerson's bail for $10,000 per indictment, and then stated for the record, "I want the proceedings to reflect even if this bail is posted, Mr. Torgerson will still be on hold for the remaining years he has left to serve for his past robbery conviction."

After this ruling, the defense moved to consolidate all four indictments. Prosecutor Mattson rose in protest. "Our Supreme Court has ruled in a situation very similar to this. Each victim is a singularly distinct crime. The State has a right to separate and distinct trials for each victim."

Collins countered, "My motion is simply to consolidate all four indictments into one trial to avoid what the Supreme Court has also criticized in terms of serialized prosecutions."

Judge Olson took the matter under advisement, promising he would rule on this matter at the next hearing. In his final motion, Collins asked the court to authorize the employment of two expert witnesses for the defense.

Judge Olson asked if the State had any objection to the motion and Prosecutor Mattson said, "Well, there are no names indicating who the experts are, Your Honor. The State would be very interested in knowing who these people are because the State has to go out and get a psychiatrist too. I don't want to be out looking for the same psychiatrist."

"I don't think it's any of the State's concern or business at this point who I might seek to retain as an expert defense witness," Collins retorted. "I'll give him notice of who it is far enough in advance so he can obtain the psychiatrist of his choice."

"Mr. Collins, I'm going to grant your motion," Judge Olson said. "You can employ one competent psychiatrist of your choice. But I don't want you to hire a psychiatrist from California. You can get competent people in Minnesota. The usual practice is to permit the employment of one expert witness, not two."

"My feeling is that we are not talking about an exact science, and I would like the jury to have the opportunity to compare comments or conclusions of more than one competent psychiatrist, if that is at all possible," Collins said. "I would feel more comfortable being able to rely on more than one."

Judge Olson scowled. "I'm only going to allow one. The defendant is not claiming he is not competent to stand trial. He's not claiming that he doesn't understand the proceedings or that he is unable to cooperate with counsel, is he?"

"He's not making that claim at this time, Your Honor."

"Is that correct, Mr. Torgerson?" the Judge asked, turning toward the defendant.

"Correct," Torgerson replied.

Having been postponed by one week, the next hearing took place on September 13. This was a critical session for the court, the defense, and the prosecutor. None of them wanted to risk making a mistake that might send the case into appeal.

Mattson asked the court to determine whether Torgerson was competent to stand trial. Judge Olson decided to make a determination of competency after he received a report from a professional psychiatrist. Next, defense counsel Collins opened a discussion about the use of these subsequent expert reports.

"As the court and county attorney well realizes, this case involves indictments charging offenses of the greatest degree of gravity," Collins said, stepping out from his table. "I need to be in a position of advising my client what the procedure is going to be, that he's going to be discussing these things in confidence with psychiatrists or clinical psychologists. I can't advise him as to what attitude he should take without this assurance.

"I really need to be able to advise him in advance what use is going to be made of the reports. The sole purpose of this motion is to determine whether Mr. Torgerson is presently mentally ill or mentally deficient so as to be incapable of understanding these proceedings.

"Since our last court appearances there have been additional factors have given me enough basis to believe a serious question does exist with regard to Mr. Torgerson's capacity to proceed in this prosecution. I need to be able to let him know his rights are going to be protected—that he will receive the complete report rather than just simply blank opinions or conclusions."

Mattson countered. He insisted psychiatrists could assist the court by determining if the defendant is capable of understanding the proceedings and by showing whether or not Torgerson had homicidal tendencies. Mattson said, "Because of this, your Honor, I request the report be open and of use to the prosecution."

"If that is the case," Collins retorted, "I will advise my client not to cooperate with any psychiatrist. The relationship has to be confidential."

"Well, I think you understand, Mr. Collins," Judge Olson interjected, "that the referred psychiatrist is going to get on the stand. He must be allowed to testify to some of the facts. You and your client waive them."

"For what purpose, Your Honor? For his competency or to determine the prosecution on the merits?"

"I think for all purposes. I think that is the posture of the law."

"That he is waving any privilege he has?" Collins said, in an incredulous voice

"If the statements made to the doctor are then used in a hearing here," Judge Olson said, "and the doctor is allowed to testify to those factual statements—the one's that the defendant made to him—at that moment privilege goes out the window. We can't let a person select what facts he wants to have exposed and which ones he wishes to conceal."

"That's what I'm trying to guard against," Collins said. "I'm trying to give him that freedom."

The judge sighed. "Ordinarily, I put in the order that any statements the person makes to the examining psychiatrist cannot be used in a subsequent criminal proceeding to determine guilt or innocence. This is what I will put in the order: the statements he makes to the psychiatrist cannot be used against him in a trial to determine guilt or innocence. But, if he decides to use the psychiatrist as a witness, he waves privilege."

After ordering that the psychiatric reports would be filed with the court and each attorney, the court stipulated specific conditions that had to be followed in making the psychiatric evaluation. Next, Judge Olson turned to the selection of the psychiatrist. He suggested using the staff at the Rochester State Hospital and specifically recommended Dr. Tyce.

Both attorneys simultaneously stood to object.

"Mr. Torgerson has previously been a patient of that institution," Collins said. "I would like to feel that the examination would be absolutely objective—without any possibility of carry over impressions from previous evaluations or examinations."

"Your Honor, the State would also have an objection because of the background. Dr. Tyce was involved in some of the previous hearings. As I understand it, he (Torgerson) has been out there and everything because of his release from a mental institution before.

"I would rather see a separate, independent psychiatrist that hasn't had any contact before or that might be involved…"

Collins nodded in agreement.

Judge Olson stipulated that Dr. Richard Stein, the head of psychiatry at The Mayo Clinic, would select a psychiatrist, unknown to the defendant, from his staff to conduct the mental evaluation of David James Torgerson. A week later, Torgerson's mental examination was conducted by Dr. Graf, a Mayo Clinic staff psychiatrist. His complete report was submitted to all concerned parties: Judge Olson, Defense Counsel Collins and Prosecutor Mattson.

36

The parties met again on October 26, 1973. Judge Olson asked if either side had additional information to submit before the court made a determination concerning Torgerson's competence to stand trial. Prosecutor Mattson indicated the State was willing to rely on the court's judgment. Defense counsel Collins demurred, "I assume the court's determination this morning is going to focus on the part of the report where Dr. Graf gives his opinion that Mr. Torgerson does meet the legal standards with regard to competency to stand trial. That he does understand the proceedings against him and can participate in his defense.

"I would be remiss if I did not state this six page report goes well beyond that specific issue. At the very least, I think a fair reading of the report would lead anyone to conclude Mr. Torgerson suffers from a mental illness of a very severe nature. I think the court should take that into consideration."

"Did I understand you to say that you thought Dr. Graf was referring to some psychotic condition?" Judge Olson asked.

"I'm not stating that this report contains a definite diagnosis of psychosis," Collins replied. "But both Dr. Graf's and Dr. Schwartz's reports indicate there is evidence suggestive of psychosis."

"Alright, we'll have the record show the court received a report from Dr. Graf, of the Mayo Clinic, who states it is his opinion the defendant suffers from a mental illness, which he classifies as a personality disorder of the schizoid type as distinguished from schizophrenia, and that he believes Mr. Torgerson has the capacity to understand the proceedings against him in order to participate in his defense of criminal proceedings for murder."

Collins interrupted, "If it pleases the court, in as much as…"

Judge Olson cut him off, his eyes flashing a warning bigger than a stop sign. "I think both of you agreed the findings were to be made by the court after the referral and examination and input from all sources, right?"

Both attorneys nod, but Collins cannot restrain himself. "Dr. Schwartz's psychometric examination showed evidence of diffuse organic brain dysfunction," Collins argued. "I think that is significant. He indicates evidence of psychosis, even though that specific diagnosis has not been made. It would be terribly unfair to simply judge the defendant as competent without stipulating that there is evidence of a very severe nature of mental illness."

"This report does not, and my finding does not, relate to the mental condition of the defendant at the time of the alleged offense," Judge Olson said. "This relates to the man's present ability to stand trial. The court will take the report on those merits. This court rules the defendant is competent to stand trial."

The motion to consolidate the four indictments for murder is the court's next order of business. In the last hearing, the defense had recommended consolidation and the State opposed it. Mattson announced the State's position for the record. "These are singularly distinct and separate crimes and individual, distinct deaths, which call out for separate trials."

Collins jumped to his feet to request more time to prepare a proper response, one that would support consolidating all counts. Judge Olson advised both lawyers to have their arguments ready on the following Monday.

The next hearing became moot.

On November 6, 1973, David James Torgerson was found dead in cell block number five. On that evening, the Olmsted County Jail housed twenty-six prisoners. According to the jailer who had been on night duty, David Torgerson was the only prisoner in cell block five. In addition, he was not confined to his cell and no unusual noise was detected.

No note was found.

An official investigation into Torgerson's death was conducted by the Olmsted County Sheriff's detectives Walter Fischer and Arnold Hass. Fischer's official written statement reported:

> Mr. Torgerson tied up his own body in order to commit suicide. First, he tied his feet with silk material. Then he tied a piece of sheet around his mid-section. At that point, he tied a noose to the top of the shower. He then placed a second noose around his neck and tied his hands to the middle section of his body by looping a swath of fabric around the sheet that had been placed there. When he stepped into the shower he dropped down. He was not able to reach up with his hands to free himself and he could not lift himself up with his legs as they hung down too far below the shower.

I got access to a file marked, 'Not for public release.' It stated:

> David James Torgerson was found hanging by a piece of bed sheet from a communal shower stall. Torgerson's hands were tied one-to-the-other and then fixed through a piece of bed sheet, which was wrapped around his mid-section. His hands were secured with strips of aqua silk material, which had been cut into separate pieces or scarves, and his feet were bound by a similar glossy white fabric. These scarves were later identified as edging that came from blankets used in the jail. A piece of blue bed sheet bound Torgerson's waist. A green sheet was used for the neck noose. His feet were tied together separate from any other binds on the body.

The *Rochester Bulletin* was the first paper to report Torgerson's suicide. According to its first posting, a spokesman for the Mayo Clinic communicated that Torgerson's psychiatric evaluation had detected suicidal tendencies. The same article noted Lawrence Collins, Torgerson's defense counsel, believed the suicide to be an impulsive act. When I spoke to Lawrence Collins years later, he told me Torgerson was incapable of normal emotions such as depression.

Torgerson's death certificate listed his cause of death as suicide.

You be the judge.

I learned of David Torgerson's death from my roommate, Ann, who followed his saga in the newspaper more closely than I did. "He's dead! The asshole killed himself," she yelled at me after the news hit the paper. "I'm so glad that bastard is dead. Aren't you?"

An electric tremor moved down my spine.

"I just feel sad," I said.

That weekend I traveled home to Austin. Mom and I sat down in the front room of our three bedroom rambler. Nothing had changed: the walls were still turquoise and the furniture had not been replaced since the day we moved in a dozen years before. I perched on the footstool, which sort of matched Mom's worn, sturdy brown reading chair.

"Well, it's good that they caught him. Everything will be okay now," Mom said to me as she lit up a cigarette. She inhaled deeply and then placed her cigarette in the amber ashtray, which sat on top of the maple end table next to her chair.

"Uhmm, yeah, I suppose," I said. "You know, Mom, we've never really talked about what happened to me."

"I've been waiting for you to ask," she said while getting up from her chair. She walked down the hall and disappeared into her bedroom. I heard a dresser drawer open then close. A minute later she handed me a yellowed envelop labeled, 'Carol's Accident.' I have been saving these for you," she said.

I opened the envelop flap and removed several neatly clipped faded *Austin Daily Herald* newspaper articles that had reported my attack. I fingered each one.

"Mom, I've been wondering, why didn't you get me some help when all that happened?" I said, breaking the silence in the room.

"I didn't think you needed it," she said. "You never talked about it."

"That should have been your first clue," I sighed.

"Times were different then. It was the 1950's, Carol," she said while taking a draw on her Salem cigarette. "We knew less then—psychology was a new science. If I had taken you to a psychiatrist, people would've thought you were crazy. I didn't want to stigmatize you."

"Oh yeah, like Sybil Anderson."

"Huh? Whadda mean Sybil Anderson?"

"Oh, well, you remember we were friends in the seventh grade. But after I went to her house, her mother wouldn't let her talk to me anymore because she said I was **that** girl."

My mother's bright blue eyes flickered, and then turned to flint. "What? That fat old cow. Why didn't you tell me? I would have gone right over there and given her a piece of my mind."

"There was a lot I didn't tell you about then," I murmured.

That afternoon, I called up a high school girl friend. We made plans to meet in a basement bar located on Main Street. After we claimed a table near the action, a mini-skirted waitress approached. I ordered my standard: Cuba Libra, rum and coke with a splash of lime. A silver-mirrored disco ball spun above the snug dance floor. I tapped my foot and shook my head to the beat of Credence Clearwater's, Proud Mary. My hair hung long and heavy. I felt it bounce across my shoulders like tumbleweed skittering in the desert wind.

A guy standing at the bar caught my eye. I looked away. Took another quick glance. He put his drink down onto the bar and walked over to me. I smiled at him when he asked me to dance. Two songs later, the tempo slowed. I liked the feel of his hand on the small of my back.

"Haven't seen you before," he said. "Is this your first time?"

"Not really, but I don't come home much," I said. "I live in Minneapolis now, but I grew up in Austin. We graduated from the same class."

"Huh, I don't recognize you. What's your name?"

"Carol, Carol Haack."

He dropped both hands, twirled on his right foot and abandoned me in the middle of the dance floor without a backward glance.

By the time I found my seat, I knew he wasn't worth a second more of my time.

Epilogue

Everyone has a story. Rain falls into all of our lives. At some point, everyone copes with painful life events. A stranger stole my childhood trust and my sense of safety. His actions provided the fodder for others to whisper about me. I was cast into the darkness of being that girl. Often, victims of violent acts do not receive the help they need. This was especially true in 1959. Although today's parents would never pack their daughter off to a week of summer camp after such a traumatic event, it would be unjust to view my parents' decision under the lens of a modern spotlight. My heart would grieve if readers judged my mother harshly. Her love for me was fierce and unconditional. Her stoicism and strength held our family foundation steady. I drank from the well of her resilience as a child and throughout my adolescence. As an adult, I inherited it.

By the time I was in my twenties, I began to have flashbacks and to share my story with a few confidants. I tried to understand. In my thirties, I sought counseling for 'job burn-out' and visited this old, quiet wound. For me, this event exploded the unspoken covenant that binds child and parent. For years I buried deep in my heart the irrational belief that my father had failed to protect me. In my forties, I read every true crime book that I could get my hands on. I studied books written about the ways of serial killers. I became driven to find an explanation for the inexplicable. In my fifties, I began to write about it.

Information is power. By telling this old story, I reclaimed my power. For me, knowing all became a catalyst to healing.

Although Torgerson blamed his acts on some unknown force that just took over his life, his explicit recall of each crime scene shows his true psychopathic nature. He played through the details of his horrific murders with the obsession of a spurned lover. For a while, he disgusted me so much I ended up being in the unenviable position of wanting to kill a dead guy. Also I came to see that the system had failed us all.

Recent research suggests experts can spot psychopathy in a child as young as three or four (*Atlantic Monthly*, June 2017). In 2013, a new medical diagnostic term describes psychopathic children as having "callous and unemotional traits." According to Kent Kiehl, a psychiatrist at the University of New Mexico, if a child between eight-to-ten-years-old commits early violence alone (as David Torgerson did) an interior impulse toward harm has been set.

In addition, the brains of serial killers have been examined. Findings show the frontal lobe, which is the center of impulse control, to be smaller in remorseless killers. Perhaps brain science and juvenile research facilities will provide insight into the psychopathic brain.

Even though it costs money to keep psychopaths locked up, it costs our communities too much not to do so.

The outcome of my court case marked Torgerson, "a danger to society." When that appropriate and crucial phrase was removed from his file dozens of victims, their friends, families and our society suffered grievous loss. Violent predators such as David Torgerson cannot be rehabilitated. One way we can work toward positive change is to alter plea bargaining rules. I believe that no plea should be accepted until a thorough background check has been submitted to the court—not the other way around. If this had happened, David James Torgerson would not have been let loose on us all.

While my traumatic experience tested my spirit and endurance, it also granted insight. I came to know the ephemeral quality of life. Being ostracized was a gift that inspired me to become a more thoughtful, kind, and compassionate human being.

In the 1960s, '70s and '80s, few resources existed for survivors of violent crime. The same can be said about services for surviving family members. This gap was filled for Minnesota residents with the founding of the Victim Intervention Program Institute (VIPI) in 1997, which was developed at the request of Lieutenant Joe Corcoran, retired commander of the St. Paul Police Homicide Unit.

In 2007, VIPI changed its name to Survivor Resources. Survivor Resources serves clients with crisis response and follow-up care; provides support groups for homicide, suicide and accidental death survivors; organizes annual memorial services; and strives to educate the public and heighten their awareness to victims' plight through a variety of community presentations.

If you are a trauma survivor, you can reach out for help and understanding. Here are some web links:

www.survivorresources.org—support for survivors of traumatic loss

www.griefloss.org—grief counseling center for survivors

www.traumacenter.org–Resources to assist trauma victims and their families www.ncvc.org–National Center for Victims of Crime; resources for coping with trauma

www.afsp.org–American Foundation for Suicide Prevention; resources for coping with suicide loss

Acknowledgements

After being admitted to an MFA program at Hamline University, I began to write about my childhood trauma. While searching the microfiche at the Minnesota History Center, I found a newspaper clipping that suggested there were other girls like me—girls who were also strangers to David Torgerson. Through a serendipitous exchange with true crime writer, Ron Franscel (The Darkest Night), I was connected to Cindy Kryska, a sister of one of these other unnamed victims. We arranged to meet at a local pizza parlor. She arrived carrying a beach bag full of information about the murder of her sister and Torgerson's other victims. After we ordered a sausage pie, she placed a framed 8" x 12" high school senior picture of her dead sister, Julie, on the table between us. We could have been cousins. We wore our hair the same way—long and parted down the middle. Eventually, I would meet with and interview sisters of all of the victims. I owe deep gratitude to Cindy Kryska, Karen Nelson, Kitty Fallgren, Peggy Chihak, Belinda Hoebing, and Janice Carlson for sharing stories about their beloved sisters. I hope I have done them justice. Charlotte Jarrett, thanks for calling me back. I was touched by your pain.

I would like to thank Kasey Johanson, records supervisor of the Rochester Police Department, for her encouragement and for giving me easy access to Olmstead County police records and court transcripts. Ruth Bauer Anderson, Minnesota Historical Society reference associate, you were enormously helpful. I am grateful for your assistance in finding old records not open to the public and in accessing over 100 microfiche newspaper accounts.

I bear a huge, unpayable debt to my California writers critique group: Dotti Reis, Judith Fabris, and Mardiyah Tarantio. Judy thanks for forming our group and sticking up for me when I needed it most. Your hawkish editing eye always served me well. Mardiyah, you showed me how to be poignant and funny at the same time. I remember more than once saying I don't know how to write such and so. I can still hear your graceful French accent: "Yes, you do, Care-ol." You always provided just the right example to tug on my brain. Dotti, long after you were gone, your voice floated across the rose planted in your honor, "There must be some way to make the title about the girls…" I miss you so.

Karen Bronshteyn, librarian and friend extraordinaire, thanks for all of your resourceful help.

Cheerleading from Kate Kennel, Barb Keller, Nancy Gale, Priscilla Swatosh, Sharon Schrafel, Jeff Anderson and Ted Haack kept me moving forward.

I also want to acknowledge my Arizona AAUW book group members: Kathy Lopez, Claudia Greenwood, Bobbi Nall, Kat Cooper, Deb Dilllon, Ellie Laumark, Sara DeRouchey, Marlene Walsh, Julie Pavari, and Tracy Smiles. Thanks for your added encouragement. Linda Williams, I appreciate your proof-reading diligence. I want to thank Betsy Amster, Los Angeles agent for salient advice about putting the book in chronological order. I wasn't ready to hear it back then, but I never forgot it. You were right.

Finally, thank you, Bonnie Gelep. You are the goddess of punctuation, a patient teacher, and my forever friend.

> *What was Taken* would never have materialized without all of this support. I am grateful.

About the Author

Carol Haack, a former teacher at St. Paul and Anoka colleges in Minnesota, now lives in the peaceful bluffs of Arizona. Interested readers can contact her at: verbatim063@yahoo.com

Posted reviews are encouraged and welcomed.

www.ingramcontent.com/pod-product-compliance
Lightning Source LLC
Chambersburg PA
CBHW071653090426
42738CB00009B/1505